"WW III has already begun and we aren't even aware of it."

WINNING THE WAR AGAINST RADICAL ISLAM,
By Dr. Robert A. Morey, Page 122, Christian Scholars Press, 2002
ISBN 193 123 0080

Manhattan Massacre

By

Brian James Shanley

ISBN: 1-4033-8836-9 (e-book)
ISBN: 1-4033-8837-7 (Paperback)

This book is printed on acid free paper.

1stBooks - rev. 01/28/03

PREFACE

I'll never forget the first time I knew that there was a problem here in America. It was in either late 1990 or early 1991 and I was in my 8th grade classroom at Maria Sanford Junior High School in Minneapolis, MN. I didn't care about religion at all yet back then, and was just beginning to take an interest in politics and current issues. Studying world events was an exciting thing to me.

America had sent military troops over to Saudi Arabia to come against Saddam Hussein's forces of Iraq. All I knew at that time (I was 14) was that it was about freeing Kuwait from a sicko. That was the extent of my knowledge of Operation Desert Shield (later called Operation Desert Storm). But it was enough for me to feel proud to be an American, and proud to come from a country that fought for the cause of freedom all around the world.

Since it was clear to any thinking person that our nation's military troops were heroes, I assumed that my classmates around me were just as proud to be from America as I was. I mean, they had access to the same information that I did. I voiced my opinion about how proud I was of our troops at school in my daily speech, without even thinking that anyone would or could hold to an opposing viewpoint.

My excitement and patriotism, however, were soon met with opposition by some of my fellow students at lunch hour. One of the kids at the lunch table was American-born, but saw Momar Khadafi as a hero! He said he wanted to grow up to be just like him! Another of the kids at my table was not American-born, but had come from a country somewhere in either East Africa or the Middle East. He disagreed with me and said that America was not heroic, but arrogant! He saw us as bullies. I shortly thereafter suggested that if he did not like it here, he should return to wherever he came from. I don't know what ever became of these two guys after junior high. I never saw them again after that school year.

Minneapolis was a diverse town, even back then. There was a great variety of people that made up our student body. And about the issue of the war in Iraq, there was no shortage of opinions. I was not surprised to hear a variety of opinions, suggestions, and thoughts about the war. But I *was* shocked to hear the high amount of anti-American sentiment that as in the air at my school.

Most people who came out and openly expressed hatred for our nation were immigrants who had been here for only a few months. But there were also some who had been in America for their whole lives, as had several generations of their family before them. Their professed anti-American stances I chalked up to ignorance, bad home training, and having a bad life up to that point. People of this mind set were usually very bitter and angry individuals.

But this problem (having citizens of our country who hated it, while living here as citizens at the same time) really became visible for me one day in a classroom. We were discussing the war in Iraq, and patriotism was the minority view among the students! The majority of the kids alongside me were against the war and had some problem or another with our country in general. Some were actually pulling for Saddam Hussein and Iraq to win the war! I was disgusted.

After things got too irrational and the teacher had lost all control of the classroom, my mind began to wander. I stared out the classroom window at the street outside. I thought about the future. Every motivational speaker that came to our school auditorium had constantly reminded us that we were America's future. I wondered if the adults who were calling us the future knew what kind of people they were saying that to. Did they know, as they stood up on the stage and addressed us, how much anger was being taught to some of us at home? Did these people know how much anti-American anger was sitting right at their feet? Did they even really care? Probably not.

I read a magazine article in our school library later on that month and learned that my school was not alone in producing people like this. My city, Minneapolis, was not the only major city in America with this problem in it. There were people like this in many large cities all over our country. The underground pro-Iraq and the anti-American view was bigger than I had first feared, especially in cities with a large number of immigrants who had arrived from the Middle East.

Our country was sitting on a time bomb. More people who thought like this and hated our country were arriving onto our soil every month. They were not turned away or even questioned. Even if they were coming over from a country that was notorious for hating America, their individual backgrounds were not investigated thoroughly and they were welcome with open arms. Many were even given government money, like welfare, to live on as they got their new life started here. Yet, since I was going to school alongside them, I got to hear first-hand how many of them had anger towards our country. What was going to happen if they became too large numerically and too powerful financially inside of our country one day?

I thought it was a bunch of politically-confused immigrants and a few angry Americans who just didn't know America's whole story correctly. What I did not know back then was that all of these people shared a common bond - a certain religious world and life view. I did not know that this style of thinking, in which America is seen as some bully slapping around little countries, was actually implanted by the leaders of an evil religion.

All I knew was that for some reason, America was home to a growing number of people who hated it - and they all seemed to be in my town. To find fanatical nuts who wanted our country to crumble, I no longer had to turn on the evening news and see a reporter interviewing a terrorist dictator on the other side of the world. I merely had to leave home and walk the streets of my city. I simply had to show up to school and have a conversation with certain classmates. It was easy to see that if more and more people of this mindset showed up every day continually, and if more and more Americans trained their kids to think this way, in the future this movement would present a major problem to our country.

It was at this time that I first knew that there was a national threat of some kind here in America. There was a ticking time bomb on our very own streets. This was back in 1991. Even back then, I could tell that whatever this issue was, if not dealt with and left alone or ignored, it'd hurt us in a big way one day.

10 years later this problem, having been left totally ignored and having been allowed to grow tremendously, came back to haunt us as a nation. While Christian churches were interested in building coffee shops instead of evangelizing Muslim neighborhoods, our nation was infiltrated by people under the influence of a false and evil god. While our Congress was busy passing laws about building bigger sports stadiums, our country was being set up. While our educational institutions and work places were busy shoving post-modern diversity teachings down our throats, room was being made at the table in everyone's minds for systems of belief and thought whose goal was to overthrow our own government. We as a country dropped the ball totally for an entire decade, making it easier for haters of our nation to move into place and prepare for a strike against us. One might even go so far as to call our leaders and teachers enablers and, therefore, indirect participants.

The anti-American sentiment that I had seen in seed form as a kid had bloomed into a black rose of evil and destruction. Those who hated our country were done talking and were done spreading their message *verbally*. It was now time for *action*. And they acted by carrying out one of the most vile acts possible - the mass murder of innocent people.

The news tells us that it was just a bunch of fanatics. The attack was just a 1-time deal that will never happen again. All we have to do is invade Afghanistan, find the problem people, and take them out. All we have to do then is go to war with Iraq again, and this time force a regime change from Hussein to something else.

But the truth is much deeper and the solution is much more complex than that. Something uglier than radical fanaticism was the motivational factor that moved in the hearts of the criminals who have attacked our country. And something much closer to home than we think was behind it. Invading another country cannot help us if the problem is actually here! If we fail to see this ugly thing for what it really is, then we will fail to deal with it. If we fail to deal with it, then life as we once knew it here in America is already gone forever.

Picture a new way of life here in America. A new reality in which you sit down in the evening after a long day of work and eat dinner. You flip on the nightly news and you see a report of a random shooting spree inside of a McDonald's restaurant. Or you see a report of a suicide bomber wearing a bomb under his coat, and letting it explode in a Wal-Mart store. You hear of shopping malls being evacuated because of bomb threats. You hear of a nuclear device ripping through the downtown area of a major city. Picture not being shocked at all, because it happens so often and the news is full of things like this every day. Now picture this not being a story about what is taking place in a Middle Eastern country, but right here in America!

We have been going down the road towards just such an environment for over 20 years. Right now as I write this, it is still early enough to stop this from coming to pass. There is still time to reverse the trend. But this will not always be the case. Time will not always be on our side. We're dealing with a finite amount of time and a limited window of opportunity in which to move. America needs to stop talking and start acting. And we need to do it now, while our country still stands.

There is something evil at work that has set itself up against America and against America's people. It will be against us in a long campaign, lasting over many decades. It has already been here for decades in the past, and will still continue its efforts either until we deal with it, or until it accomplishes its plans against us.

September 11th, 2001 was not an isolated incident. It was not a 1-time event. It was just the beginning.

On that date and every day since, America has been on full alert. Well, this author has been on full alert since 1997! If you've never studied this issue before, you owe it to yourself to read what I have written in this book. **_"MANHATTAN MASSACRE"_**. That day was bad enough. Let's work together to prevent the next one.

TABLE OF CONTENTS

PREFACE V

A PERSONAL WORD FROM JOE ERVIN XV

DEDICATION xvii

INTRODUCTION xix

CHAPTER ONE
SEEN COMING A MILE AWAY 1

CHAPTER TWO
THE DAY AMERICA STOOD STILL 19

CHAPTER THREE
ISLAM'S CLOSE RELATIONSHIP TO TERRORISM 36

APPENDIX A
The Muslim Concept Of Heaven As A Motivational Factor Which Results In Acts Of Terrorism 127

APPENDIX B
Roots: Why They Hate Us So Much 149

APPENDIX C
Resources: Equipping Christians To Take Action 171

APPENDIX D
Morey's Radical Suggestion -"TOUGH LOVE" 183

A PERSONAL WORD FROM JOE ERVIN

Prior to September 11th 2001, the black cauldron of Islam had been brewing for quite sometime, gaining acceptance throughout the nation from various organizations, be they secular or religious. Since September 11th 2001, many people here in America are scrambling to find out what happened. And many Islamic scholars, politicians, and yes, even some Christian ministers, are coming out of the woodworks in an attempt to explain and justify this mess.

Those that come out against Islam have been silenced and given very little, if any, airplay. Franklin Graham, the son of evangelist Billy Graham, was blasted for commenting on the wickedness of Islam. So was Pat Robertson. The thing I noticed was that when these men were called upon to explain their position, they were often times presented by the media in such a way that made them come across to the masses as being unloving towards Muslims or anti-Muslim.

This book is important for many reasons, mostly because the victims of 9-11-01 and their families deserve an explanation for why these terrible events have taken place. It is sad that they have been given nothing but poor excuse after poor excuse by the government and media, which is why this book couldn't have come at a better time. With the attacks on the WTC and Pentagon, people are being misguided and fed a Sunday school version of Islam. This book will serve to set the record straight once and for all, getting down to the crux of the matter, which is the Islamic teaching of Jihad (holy war).

Brian James Shanley has been studying and doing research on Islam and it's effects on our culture since 1997. He has been on the front lines, sounding the alarm here in Minnesota well before it ever became popular to do so. He has debated many Muslims and non-Muslims alike on the street, in the work place, and in the church concerning the violent nature of Islam. It is my hope that at the very least, this book will plant a seed of curiosity in those who read it and force them to seek further truth concerning the true nature of Islam.

Joe Ervin
2002

<u>DEDICATION</u>

This writing is dedicated to the memory of those innocent people who were lost on this horrible date in American history. I tried to tell people it was coming before it did, but the world thought I was crazy and mean for talking about it.

It is also dedicated to those brave men and women on the New York City Police Department and Fire Department who gave their lives while attempting to save others.

And finally, it is dedicated to those citizens in America who have been searching for the answer as to why the attack happened. It is the intent of this book to finally give you the truth that the politicians and the media refuse to supply you with. I hope it removes the blindfolds from people's eyes and allows them to see the truth, even if the truth may seem to be too difficult to handle.

God bless America.

Brian James Shanley

<u>INTRODUCTION</u>

Every so often an ugly disaster of unimaginable horror and great tragedy takes place. The date it happens is forever etched into the minds and onto the hearts of the people who are alive in the time in which it occurs. In 1912 it was the sinking of the Titanic. In 1941 it was the attack of Pearl Harbor. In 1963 it was the assassination of President John F. Kennedy. In 1986 it was the explosion of the Space Shuttle Challenger. In 1995 it was a bomb going off in downtown Oklahoma City, OK.

Whatever generation of person you are talking to determines the particular disaster through which they lived. If they were old enough to comprehend what happened, often times they can remember it like it just happened yesterday - even if it really happened decades ago. They can tell you exactly where they were and what they were doing at the moment they heard about it.

These events cause ripples in time that change our lives and forever alter the course of history. Going forward after these disasters, nothing is the same.

And I'm sad to say that our generation is no exception. Wherever you were and whatever you were doing, you will never forget the moment that you heard America had been attacked. It was Tuesday morning, September 11th, 2001.

If I live to be 100 I will never fail to remember that day. I was at my desk at my job in the secular work place. I worked for Wells Fargo Home Mortgage in the Minneapolis

Service Center (at that time it was located in a suburb called Bloomington). My good friend Joe Ervin emailed me and asked, *"Did you hear about New York?"*

I wrote back and said, *"No. What happened?"*

He said, *"Two planes crashed into the two twin towers of The World Trade Center. The World Trade Center isn't even standing anymore."*

If it had been **one plane**, my response would have been, *"What a tragic accident"*. But since there were **two planes** hitting the World Trade Center I knew it was not an accident. So I replied, *"It was the Muslims."*

I went around my job telling people about what had happened. And I gave them my own personal take - that our Muslim community here in America had finally hit us from the inside like they had always been talking about doing. I was able to tell my co-workers all about it in detail, using terms like "jihad" and "Osama Bin Laden" before they became household words. This was because I had studied this issue for years before, and was watching and waiting for an event like this to happen. All the while, I had been praying to be wrong about the issue. I did not want a tragedy to take place, and had been doing what I could to warn people about the Islamic threat all over the streets of my city.

But people were still in shock and disbelief. They were having enough trouble accepting the fact that it had happened. To try and say for sure who did it or why was bigotry as far as they were concerned. To some I was a jerk who was finger-pointing at a particular group, because I must have had some personal problem against the people that make up the group.

But to those who had known me for a while before the attack, it was very familiar. It was the fulfillment of everything I had been talking about for the preceding 4 years. Even to this day I'll be hanging out at a mall or something, and a person that I haven't seen in years comes up to me and says, *"Ever since September 11th, 2001 I've been thinking about you. You were right. How did you know?"*.

On that day our job was evacuated and we were sent home early. Since everyone everywhere was in full panic mode nation wide, every business was closed down. There was nowhere for me to go but home. I turned on the news and was surprised to see that they were actually calling it an *attack* as opposed to an *accident*. A small part of me got happy, because I thought that perhaps the media might actually be responsible about communicating the truth of this incident to the American people.

I saw the actual footage of the planes hitting the towers for my first time. I saw the death and the chaos on the street below. It was a horrible scene to say the least. I was moved to tears.

A that time, I was in the middle of writing a book called *"QUR'ANIC CHAOS"* in which I was going to demonstrate that God had nothing to do with the authorship of the The Qur'an. Since God was not behind it, The Qur'an has no authority. And since The Qur'an has no authority, then Islam is a false religion. It was going to be a great book that was going to wake the Christian community up to the Islamic threat that hangs over the inner-city Christian church like a black cloud. It was going to teach Christians how to answer Islam, and teach lost Muslims the truth of the Gospel of Jesus Christ.

It was in my original plans, however, to only address the doctrine of jihad in one paragraph or two. I wanted mainly to stick strictly with the tons of errors in The Qur'an in other categories – like history, grammar (Muslims claim it is written in *perfect* Arabic), theology, etc. But after this event, it became necessary that I put out a writing about the issue of jihad all by itself, for the purpose of educating people that normally don't deal with issues of theology and world religions.

The real need for my authorship of this book did not come from the attack itself. It came from President Bush's and the media's irresponsible handling of the truth of the motivation that fueled the attack. What was the attack against America which took place on that day *really* about? Do you have the courage to find out? If so, then enjoy reading this. May it open your eyes to the truth, and may it motivate you to take action in order to prevent other attacks of the same size against our beloved nation that are coming soon.

BRIAN JAMES SHANLEY
2002

CHAPTER ONE

SEEN COMING A MILE AWAY

Brian James Shanley

GOD PROTECTED ME FROM ACCEPTING A LIE

In 1997 I was solicited by a Muslim and invited to accept Islam as my religion. I was excited to read everything about it that I could get my hands on. I even attended a meeting at the University of Minnesota called *"Muhammad In The Bible, Jesus In The Qur'an"*, given by my great Muslim friend Hisham. I was fascinated by the apparently strong case that was made for Islam to be seen as the truth from the True God. I did some hanging out in the Muslim community here in Minneapolis. I ordered some literature by Ahmed Deedat over the internet that was mailed to me from New York. Over that stretch of time I got a truly good look at the religion of Islam. I had the opportunity to learn things about the religion that the average person not only does not know, but does not even care to know.

Through it all God's hand was upon me, protecting me from receiving the message of Muhammad. It never did sit well with me for some reason. In 1998, after much research and truth seeking, I went on to accept the truth from the One True God of The Bible and became a Christian.

THEN HE CALLED ME TO ANSWER THE LIE

Going forward, my brief flirtation with the religion of Islam from times' past would always stay with me. You see, I had learned some horrifying things about Islam and what Islam plans to do here on the North American continent. I had learned that they have a time deadline that they are working against - a goal that they are trying to achieve by a certain targeted date. It is their goal to make Islam the dominant religion in the inner-city area of every major American city by 2013. The idea is that if they can conquer the urban areas first, the sub-urban areas will fall nice and easily. The people in the suburbs tend to follow the cultural trends that originate in the cities.

I had also learned that once they became the dominant religion in our land, they wanted to use that majority status to cause changes in our system of government, and ultimately change everything about life as we know it here in America. They just have to become the majority numerically first.

And so from 1998 on I began sounding the alarm, letting people know what I had learned. I told Christian pastors and lay people. I even told unbelievers and cultists (people who adhere to non-Christian religions)! Basically, I warned anyone who would listen. I let people know that war had been declared on America from within. The average person walking the street to and from work every day did not know it, or even care about it. It sounded too far-fetched when I told them. But their desire to ignore the problem did not make the problem go away. We were sitting on a time bomb.

THE WARNINGS WERE REJECTED

The average Christian was involved in a church that was asleep (spiritually) and did not care. They were too busy planning their youth group's next bowling trip or the next church picnic. The average lay person was busy trying to fall on the floor and shake violently like a fish out of water, thanks to an out-of-control charismatic movement. They were too poor to go into ministry with me to answer the Islamic threat because they had given all of their money to some of the "preachers" on television, waiting for a blessing they had been tricked into believing that God somehow owed them.

Most people were so focused on the quality of music being sung from the *choir microphone* that they had stopped caring about the quality of the preaching being spoken into the *preacher's microphone*! Pastors were too busy preaching messages about women wearing makeup and kids seeing the wrong movie. Many were irresponsibly drawn into the Y2K sensationalist hype as well, and even preached sermons about it! What a shameful and embarrassing portion of Christian church history that I had to witness before my eyes!

No matter who I was talking to, with the exception of a few scattered individuals who actually believed me, most people thought I was a paranoid nut. I did get a few who would listen for laughs or some who would listen for entertainment (as though I was a fictional story teller) to kill time. Some people thought I was a racist who had a problem with people of Middle Eastern descent, or with the

Somali population of my town, or with other groups that the secular world would call "minorities". But very few people actually took me seriously.

GOD FINALLY SENT ME A CO-LABORER

In late 2000, God ordered my steps in such a way that I was brought across the path of an old school mate of mine, Joe Ervin. Joe & I hooked up and we decided that if Islam was seeking to become the dominant religion in every major city in America, *it was going to have to get through us* before taking The Twin Cities (Minneapolis and St. Paul, MN). We spent all of 2001 warning people about Islam's astounding growth. We told people how urgent things were becoming.

A WARNING LETTER FROM DR. BOB

Every Christian who is a student of The Bible has a favorite commentator or a favorite author. I am no exception. Mine is Dr. Robert Morey. I will mention him again later, but for now let me just say that he is the founder of Faith Defenders out of Orange, CA. In or around February or March of 2001 he sent out a letter to everyone on his ministry's mailing list. I'm sure Dr. Morey won't mind if I reproduce an excerpt of it for you to read. This was a chilling warning and a call to action that moved me personally. He had just, in the paragraph before this one, described what it had been like being a Bible college student back in the 1960's. He had just finished telling about how the Urban Missions Conferences he attended back then inspired the crowd to go out in the name of Jesus and be an effective witnessing tool in the hands of God. Then, in contrast to those events that motivated Christians:

"This last month, a different student conference assembled in Islamabad, Pakistan. But instead of a few thousand students gathering to celebrate life and salvation, over 200,000 students from all over the world assembled to celebrate death and destruction. The keynote message was given by none other than the international terrorist, Osama Bin Laden!

The most wanted terrorist in the world, Bin Laden challenged the 200,000 Muslim students to dedicate their lives to committing acts of terrorism against the Great Satan, America, and the other Western 'Christian' nations. In other words, you, your family, your church and your nation were marked for destruction by Bin Laden.

Bin Laden's speech inspired the next generation of suicide bombers and assassins to jump to their feet in applause as they committed their lives and fortunes to a Jihad against the West. The excitement and joy were overwhelming.

What should concern you is that these students represent the next generation of leaders in Muslim countries. They are the educated, well-to-do who have the money to commit themselves to terrorism.

What should also concern you is that there were American Muslim students who attended this terrorist conference who committed themselves to destroy America. They are a ticking time bomb in the heart of this country and can be set off by Bin Laden when he is ready to start a waive of death and destruction."

From this letter it was apparent to me that Dr. Morey had gotten the inside word that Islam was going to do something from inside of America. Since it was a new year and the beginning of 2001, I began to get the feeling that whatever was coming would be not only huge, but it would come before 2001 was over. So now, like the Muslims who wanted to convert the inner cities by 2013, Joe Ervin & I too had a time deadline that we were racing against. We had a finite (limited) amount of time to work with in our warnings to people before immeasurable disaster was going to hit us, probably in some heavily-populated civilian area.

THE DAY WE HAD DREADED FINALLY ARRIVED

America was blasted. I'm sure I don't have to tell you about it. The loss of life was huge. The damage was ridiculously expensive. The chaos was scary. The tragedy will be felt forever.

THOSE IN POWER RUSHED TO PUT BLINDFOLDS OVER THE EYES OF ANYONE WHO WOULD WEAR THEM

The media and the government got together as a tag team to make sure that you and I, the average citizens, didn't receive enough information to be able to panic. People were steadily indoctrinated to believe that this act of terror was done by a select group of people and, once they removed this select group of people from power in Afghanistan, life could go back to the way it was before here in America. The trick is older than dirt. Always blame one person or one small group, eliminate that person or that small group, and then everything is fine and the civilian population is calm once again.

Our government either cannot see the truth, will not see the truth, or thinks that we, the common people, are like children and could not swallow the truth, so they'll never give it to you. That's why the authorship of this book became necessary.

The truth is that we can never go back to how things were before that fateful day. As a matter of fact, even before 09-11-2001 I never thought we were safe or invulnerable from an attack to begin with. It had been building for a long time and I was not alone in feeling it coming on for years beforehand.

THE WRONG NATIONAL APPROACH IS BEING USED

Going over to Afghanistan with our armed forces to wipe out the small group that the government and the media have scape-goated will accomplish nothing except using the greatest military on the face of the earth to slap around and conquer a small nation about the size of Texas. It's not going to eliminate the problem.

You see, there cannot be a *political* solution to the problem because the problem is not *political* in nature. The problem is actually *spiritual.* And since today (in 2002) there is a Universalist commander-in-chief running the show (I know I'm stepping on someone who really believes Bush is a Christian), no one in the national power structure is even in a position to know how to properly respond. They're choosing to ignore the truth that the problem is not "terrorism" in general, but it is specifically *ISLAM*!

Islam is the motivation of the terrorism. Until we see that, we will continue to chase our tails and wonder why we didn't see the most recent attack coming. Yet we'll still want to give off an appearance like we know what we're doing and we've got it all under control. Who knows what we'll do after we clean house in Afghanistan? Will we begin to mess with Iraq? Pakistan? Who knows? Nothing would surprise me except if we actually did what we need to do. That is what would surprise me. Our national leaders seem to want to pin the attacks on anything and anyone other than Islam.

But the truth is still the truth, whether it fits into our national political correctness movement or not. And for some reason, right now our leaders are not accepting the truth and are fighting the wrong enemy. This is not Vietnam. This is not Korea. This time, our enemy is not in some other country. Our enemies are right here. They are showing up onto American soil in big numbers every single day. Going over to other countries to look for the enemies will not help us, because their soldiers have already landed in our land! We just choose not to see them.

THIS IS NOT JUST ANOTHER 90 – DAY WONDER BOOK

After the attacks happened, I watched in disgust as Christian and secular authors alike jumped on the Islamic "band wagon" and began to flood the market with all kinds of literature. And this was *after* the attack, by the way! Beforehand when I was trying to warn people ahead of time through Bible tracts and word of mouth on the streets of my town, no one wanted to hear me! Now that what I have warned about has finally taken place, it is suddenly the "in" thing to talk about.

People like the late (and great) Dr. Walter Martin and Dr. Norman L. Geisler and Abdul Saleeb and John Ankerberg and John Weldon and Dave Hunt and others had been on the mission field to Muslims for decades beforehand - even before I was born!

People like Dr. Robert Morey and William Lane Craig and Anis Shorrosh had already debated the biggest names in the Islamic academic world and exposed Islam for what it really is. These people are heroes of the Christian faith and true confronters of evil. After the trend-followers have moved on to the next big issue, these *REAL* soldiers will be right here, still continually dealing with the ancient enemy of Christianity and freedom, which is Islam.

And when some TV evangelist or some talk show host who has never cared about Islam before suddenly is an overnight expert and writes a book about Islam, it makes a mockery out of the great work that the above-mentioned people have already been doing. The people who emerge out of nowhere to get rich off of the newest trend in our culture often borrow from the above-mentioned heroes' work and never even give them credit! I find this an outrageous shame.

As an author, this is my first book. But may it never be said that I am one of the people who are ripping people off or, God forbid, one of those hucksters who want to profit off of the recent tragedy. I fully admit that my knowledge of Islam, second only to reading Islam's Qur'an itself, comes from the above-named Christian heroes' works and from other books about Islam that I have read. And I fully intend to give credit where credit is due. But I also feel a strong need to remove myself or separate myself from the people who are putting out a book about Islam strictly because it is a hot topic right now. This is sin as far as I am concerned.

Anyone who knows me knows that in late 1999 I began writing a Bible tract called "EXODUS FROM MECCA" which later became a book called "QUR'ANIC CHAOS" and then it was changed to "TERRIBLE TUESDAY" before becoming what you are reading now, "MANHATTAN MASSACRE". While it has taken a long time to get into print due to format changes as well as personal issues, the study of Islam is nothing new to me. It certainly is not a subject that I have jumped onto because it became popular. As my career as a Christian author progresses over the coming years, you will see that this will probably be *one of several books* I write about Islam. I'll even be answering Islam after it goes out of style in the culture, because my concerns about it are actually real.

Rest assured that you are not reading the work of a trend follower by working your way through this book! Ask anyone who has been around me in the past 5 years and they'll tell you.

You are not reading the work of a man who will quote others without giving them their due credit. There are enough authors like that out there already.

You are reading the work of a man who is grateful to the warriors of the Christian faith who went before him onto the battlefield to fight Islam, and will point you towards their work whenever possible. And you are reading the work of a man who is sincere in his desire to wake people up to the truth of what is going on in our country.

Brian James Shanley

YOU DESERVE TO KNOW THE TRUTH

In the rest of this book you will read irrefutable documentation that, contrary to what's being circulated today, Islam *does* teach violence. Non-Muslims are the targets and intended victims of this violence.

Muhammad's teachings are forever preserved in The Qur'an. Muhammad is more qualified than George W. Bush to say what Islam teaches, because Muhammad systematized Islam and Bush did not. And I'm more qualified than George W. Bush to say what Islam teaches, because I have studied Muhammad's writings in The Qur'an and he has not. So before gulping down what he (Bush) or any other politician is trying to feed you, I hope you will take into consideration what I have written here.

You will gain more from this book than from attending one of those trendy and popular inter-faith gatherings. These things are becoming dangerously popular - you know the kind - where on the stage you have a Buddhist monk, a Muslim Imam, a "Christian minister", a Roman Catholic priest, a witch, an American Indian shaman, an African witch doctor, and all kinds of other people running the show. Their intent is to get all people of all world religions together to pray to what they call the "universal deity". Meetings of this kind, whether in the public square or on the university campus, are all cheap theatrics and showmanship. They are fake. You won't leave a meeting of this kind knowing anything more about the attacks of September 11th, 2001 than you knew when you came in. It won't answer any of the questions that you have about the attacks. All you will have accomplished is having wasted 2 or 3 hours of your time.

This was an ugly day in American history. You are a thinking person. You have real and intelligent questions about what happened and why. Don't you think you deserve to have your curiosity satisfied? If there is a real threat out there - even if the threat is only *possibly* real, don't you think you owe it to yourself and your family to at least have some knowledge about it? I'm pretty sure that if (and when) another such attack happens, that it is not your intent to be among the people looking around in the chaotic aftermath asking "*Why?*"!

SEPTEMBER 11th, 2001 WAS THE LOGICAL END OF THE RELIGION OF ISLAM

Is Islam really a religion of peace? Yes, it is a religion of peace. Not of *peace*, but of *piece*. It's a piece of you laying on one block and another piece of you laying on the ground 3 blocks away. It's a piece of a burning building crashing down onto an innocent person. So yeah, in that sense I guess a case could be made for the peacefulness (or should I say, piecefulness) of the religion of Islam! Ha, ha, ha! The end result of Islam is disorder and chaos as everything blows up into pieces, and people are mangled and ripped into pieces.

As you enter into the rest of this book, just remember that this author was one of a very few people who were not surprised by the attack of September 11th, 2001. I was not among the people running around chaotically throughout the nation asking *"Why?"* I didn't have to. I already knew why. And I can also say with sadness that something just like it will happen again. How do I know? Because this date of September 11th, 2001 was not an isolated incident. It was just the beginning.

This was not a few misguided fanatics. It was Islam's "holy" book being carried out by real Muslims who knew exactly what they were doing. When it happens again, please don't be surprised by it. This book is attempting to sound the alarm. If you were in the majority and were caught off guard on September 11th, 2001, I have good news for you. You do not have to be caught off guard by the next one. Perhaps you can even be used by God as an instrument to help prevent it!

18

CHAPTER TWO

THE DAY AMERICA STOOD STILL

THE NEWS AND THE GOVERNMENT WORK TOGETHER TO GIVE THE AMERICAN PEOPLE A SMOKE SCREEN

It was bad enough that such horror had taken place. America had been attacked from inside by her own Muslim community. It had resulted in the deaths of thousands of innocent people.

But then the problem was added to by news anchor men and women who refused to give the common people something they deserve – the honest truth. The liberal media wasted no time in getting their faces in front of a camera and telling us all that the ones who had attacked our country were not true Muslims, but much the opposite, were a small minority group of fanatics and radicals. And of course, none of these news anchor people had the courage to interview any real experts. They didn't even interview anyone who believed differently than the view of Islam that they were trying to persuade the public to believe. Talk about bias in the media! The truth about 09-11-2001 has about as much of a chance on TV as a non-white person has in front of an angry Ku Klux Klan lynch mob!

There were a handful of us who had been studying Islam before this had ever happened, and we knew the media was lying through their teeth. Either they (the media) are extremely ignorant, or they have no problem lying to the people. Pick your choice. Either A, B, or a little of both. But either way, the facts were never made available to the people.

Some of us knew this attack was coming before it did because Islam teaches its followers to do things like this. That's why the time has never been more critical than now for me to get this book into print. If they won't tell you the truth, I will. The blindfolds need to be removed from people's eyes now while America still stands!

Was the media's story that they had put out immediately afterwards correct? Was this attack just a one-time deal that will never happen again? Was it done by people who were lacking in their understanding of The Qur'an? Or were they Muslims seeking to obey The Qur'an's commands to attack all those who are not Muslims?

Personally I believe that they were real Muslims, carrying out and obeying the teachings of Islam as found in The Qur'an. Why do I say that? You're about to find out. You're going to be surprised at the direction in which the evidence points. The idea that this was not done by real Muslims is not true at all. It was indeed done by true Muslims who knew The Qur'an well.

THE ATTACKS EXECUTED

September 11th, 2001 is a day we will never forget. On that fateful morning a group of 18 or more Muslim men went out on a dark, wicked, and evil mission in the name of Allah and, as we will read soon, in obedience to The Qur'an. They broke up into groups and attacked and hijacked 4 planes. These were regular airplanes. Just commercial flights made up of ordinary and innocent men, women, and children. Just average citizens who were in the wrong place at the wrong time.

These Muslim soldiers chose planes leaving from various East Coast cities and whose destinations were Los Angeles, CA. This was because a plane that is on a trip across the continental United States would, no doubt, be filled with maximum fuel. And on impact the more fuel, the more fire. And the more fire, the greater devastation and destruction that can be made against an intended target.

This was a carefully planned and precisely executed operation against America, which in the Middle East is called "Great Satan" by the people in Muslim countries because we have freedoms here that are not available in that part of the world. Many people hate that about us and are even jealously angry at us not only for our freedoms, but because we've always historically fought for freedom all around the world. Since Islam is opposed to freedom, then it understandable how its followers would want to stop a country that cares about spreading freedom.

These Muslims saw this attack as a jihad, or holy war, against a wicked nation. The sacred Muslim writings tell Muslims that anyone who dies in the great cause, fighting against the unbelievers (non-Mulsims) for Allah and for his messenger Muhammad, will ascend straight into paradise. They will not pass "Go". They will not collect $200 dollars. They are promised *immediate* entrance into the Muslim heaven. This, by the way, is not like the Christian concept of heaven, but is a wicked and goofy kind of heaven. I may deal with this in a future book. But this motivation is why many Muslim young people, young men and boys in particular, have no problem carrying out suicide bombings and things of that nature.

This is what the terrorists on those planes had on their minds on that now famous Tuesday morning. They wanted to strike a blow against what they perceived as an infidel (unbelieving or non-Muslim) nation, and ascend straight to paradise as payment for services rendered.

Of the 4 hijacked planes that they all took over at the same exact time, like clockwork, 2 of them were smashed in a suicide mission into 2 twin towers of a structure that once existed in New York City called The World Trade Center. The 3rd one was crashed into The Pentagon and took out a big portion of that American government building, and also killed everyone on board. And the 4th plane was possibly targeted for The White House. But inside this 4th plane some brave passengers, who had already heard about the other 3 crashes and figured that they were about to die anyway in a 4th one, rushed the terrorists. In a struggle they thwarted the plot and the plane did not make it to D.C. in order to strike The White House. The courageous passengers who fought their Muslim hijackers actually caused their plane to crash into a rural field in Pennsylvania. These people on this plane are heroes.

In New York, after having burned awhile, the 2 twin towers of The World Trade Center collapsed. They were absolutely huge buildings, the taller of the 2 being 110 stories. When they came down, they crushed thousands of people who were still stuck inside.

THE AFTERMATH

In the moments and the days that followed, there was chaos. Not just on the East Coast, but all over the nation and even in other countries. All sporting events were cancelled. No airplanes were allowed to fly over American air space. Even commercial flights were all cancelled, and people became stranded in whatever city they happened to be in at that time. The Stock Market closed. There was no postal service. Life in the busiest country on the planet had come to a stand-still. You couldn't even escape by turning the TV to your favorite TV shows because all you could receive on any channel, regular networks or cable, was live coverage of the disaster. You couldn't escape by turning on the radio, because even the Top 40 music stations were playing up-to-the-minute coverage of the latest developments of this situation.

I even remember trying to pop in a home movie to escape the media coverage. But that failed too, because the particular film I chose had been made in New York City a few years earlier, and every time they showed the skyline of that beautiful city I could see the 2 twin towers. And it made me think, "*Hmmm. Amazing. Those two buildings aren't even standing anymore*". To this day, every time I watch a movie that was shot in New York City before 09-11-2001, it has become a weird habit of mine to look for shots of the Twin Towers. Seeing the skyline now is like looking at a kid who is missing his two front teeth. There's just a gap there now that you are not used to seeing yet.

All I could do was tune into the news. It was an absolute mess. People desperately searched hospitals for their missing loved ones, praying that they were alive somewhere and not among the dead. Fire fighters and police men worked double shifts. They refused to leave the scene. They stayed behind to dig through the wreckage in hopes of finding some survivors. Some even worked to their physical limits, became exhausted, and passed out right there on the street. When they got a little sleep, woke back up, and resumed their work.

The courage of the New York City Fire and Police Departments cannot be over-stated. It was legendary and will probably go down in history. Forget about Spider Man or The Incredible Hulk. The New York City Fire Department and the NYPD are the ***real*** heroes for our kids to look up to in this generation!

THE MEDIA'S VIEW ALONE BECOMES THE ESTABLISHED WAY OF VIEWING THIS EVENT – OTHER GUESSES NOT TOLERATED

I had studied Islam for 4 years before this event happened, and I had been called all kinds of names for daring to publicize the results of my research verbally and in booklets. But now my studies became the *"in"* thing to have some knowledge about. *"Islam"* and *"jihad"* now became common words in our everyday English language, and people rushed to learn what they could about them. They wanted to be able to walk around and talk about them to show others how current and culturally aware they were of the newest fad.

In the weeks following the attack, I was concerned about how our society in general was going to view this event. My main concern was not the corporate office worker who practically lived in an office cubicle, nor was it the average "joe" struggling to make a living working in a factory, nor the teenager behind a cash register at a retail store. They were merely the *followers* of whatever the trend was going to be. I was concerned about what they'd ultimately believe because they (common people) make up the majority of our nation's people, but they were not my immediate concern at that moment.

My immediate concern at that moment was the people who occupied teaching positions in the universities and public schools. These guys were the actual *authors* of whatever the trend was going to be. These teachers would take their cues from the news media and the government.

The average working "joe" was going to follow them and the media in forming his opinion about this whole issue.

A sort of trickle-down method would allow either a right or a wrong understanding of Islam and jihad to become the dominant way of seeing things that was to be spread in our culture throughout our land.

I kept my eyes on the news media and the speeches made by the president and any other government officials. What I had feared the most began to unfold. The people's perception of Islam was being diluted with political correctness, and clouded by the modern diversity movement. A peaceful version of Islam was being passed off as though it was accurate. I had studied Islam for years before, and the picture of Islam that was being painted by the media was unrecognizable even to me!

The common cries across America were things like, *"This wasn't real Islam"* and *"Islam is not to blame"*. I wish I had a dollar every time I heard a news story whose moral was *"Don't mess with the Muslims about this incident"*. I even got called a bigot in the week following the attack for sharing the truth about Islam and jihad from The Qur'an itself with a co-worker! And this co-worker had come to me with questions about it! I could have just told them what they wanted to hear, but this would have been dishonest.

It speaks volumes about the condition of a society when lies tickle its people's ears and the truth makes them angry. In all of the confusion following this event, America was totally backwards. I could not believe what it was all coming to.

THIS BOOK IS NOTHING PERSONAL

I don't believe in attacking people or personalities. That's not what I'm all about. And I certainly don't single out Arab-Americans or our Somali brothers and sisters who have come over to call America their home. I don't want any particular group of people to feel singled out or feel like a targeted victim of this book. This book is not about people. This book is about a religion. The people exist apart from the religion. It is totally understandable and believable to suggest that a person could love *people* and have a problem with *their religion* at the exact same time.

THIS BOOK HAS NOTHING TO DO WITH THE RACIAL MAKEUP OF ANY GROUP OF PEOPLE

No one who knows me can accuse me of racism on any level. As a matter of fact, I don't even feel that Islamic Studies is a race-relations issue, no matter what the media is trying to make it into.

To be honest, calling me a racist for writing this book would be a very stupid thing to do. That charge has several problems.

Number one, if my book attacks Islam, and you call that an attack against a certain race, then you are making no distinction between a certain race of people and Islam. Right? Does it make sense? Essentially that is like saying that Islam and the race are the same, so if you attack one you attack the other. To that I can only reply that a failure to make a distinction between a race of people and Islam on the part of a critic does not automatically mean racism on my part. It just means that the critic cannot separate the 2 in his/her own mind. This is not my problem, and this does not make me a racist.

Number two, failing to make a distinction between Islam and a certain race of people is in and of itself a racist statement. It fails to recognize the diversity of the people that make up the religion of Islam worldwide. To say that attacking Islam is attacking a race of people is to identify Islam with a race of people. So calling me a racist is a racist statement, because you have to apply a racial stereotype to Islam and then identify Islam with a certain race of people, and with that race alone.

I do not recommend wasting your time trying to make such empty and bankrupt charges stick against me. Don't try to call me a bigot for daring to raise questions about Islam. That is not the case. So let us stick to the facts only, please.

As a simple point of logic, it is very possible for me to have a problem with a certain religious worldview, but at the same time love the people involved (and trapped) in the religion. As a matter of fact, this idea is so easy to understand that only people who cannot (or will not) separate a person from his/her religion will have a problem with it.

Let me just assure you that my target is not any specific group of people, but rather, I'm aimed at the spiritual forces that are guiding those people. These acts of terror were nothing more than The Qur'an being carried out to a "T". These are the teachings of Allah, which were supposedly revealed through Muhammad, and recorded in The Qur'an. We will examine them in the rest of this book.

THE MAJORITY ARE FOLLOWING AN UNEDUCATED MINORITY WHO HAVE POWERFUL POSITIONS AND TV CAMERAS

Today people are trying to defend Islam saying stuff like, "*This was done only by fanatics who aren't true Muslims.*" Of course, the people saying this are either really young and have been brain-washed by the modern diversity movement, or they're really liberal adults, or they're news anchor men and women with a social agenda of some kind, or they're on a pay roll of someone having to do with Islam.

No matter what category people fall under, whenever challenged with the question of "*How much Islamic history have you studied?*" they usually shrug their shoulders. When asked, "*How many different translations of The Qur'an do you own at your house?*" they usually look puzzled and then answer "*None*". And then when finally asked the nail-in-the-coffin question of "*How much of The Qur'an have you actually read?*", their mouths are shut.

The people who are taking a microphone and putting the innocent mask on the religion of Islam are not even qualified to speak intelligently about the issue! All they can do is vomit up the old, tired, and borrowed cliches that were fed to them at their most recent tolerance seminar on their college campus or in their work place. They can only regurgitate the catch-phrases they heard their professors spew out in their Comparative Religion course at their liberal university. But when it comes to raw facts and tangible data, they can offer you none to support their view. This should tell you something about the view they are

33

trying to feed you. If a view cannot be backed up by evidence, but only with emotionalism and slogans, then that view is more than likely not true.

THE MASSES REJECT THE TRUTH - A LIE BECOMES THE MAJORITY NATIONAL VIEW

In contrast, I have studied the issue at length. As far back as 1998 I was warning people that Islam was building for this day, right under our noses, right here on our streets in America. It was truly an inside job.

I knew an attack from within our own country was coming someday, and I even knew it'd be this big and on this level. I just could not fill in the exact blanks as to when, where, or how it would come. But people were too busy calling me "mean". People thought I was "negative" and "not loving". I got called "intolerant" and even "ignorant". This was difficult and hurt my feelings a lot. The silliest thing they ever called me was "judgmental".

It is silly to ever call anyone judgmental. You cannot call a person judgmental without first forming a judgment about them! When they said, *"You're so judgmental"* I'd respond, *"Is that the judgment that you've made about me?"* Calling someone judgmental is in and of itself a judgment about them. So this is actually not bright. Brother or sister reading this, never allow someone to call you judgmental. Expose their statement against you for the flaw that it is.

Anyway, people don't call me these names anymore too often. The name calling and the stabbing in the back, even by other Christians at times (which is an extremely painful thing to live through), has not disappeared completely, unfortunately. But for the most part, people see that there is actually something to what I have been talking about for the last few years.

To be honest, I hated to be right on this day. But I've had people who thought I was nuts prior to September 11th, 2001 apologize to me, become close friends of mine, and even volunteer to help me get the truth out! So I know people's minds can be changed once they get the facts! And I'm excited to get those facts into your hands! Woohoo! However the biggest tragedy of all is that the majority of people out there don't want to hear the truth. If you do, keep on reading.

CHAPTER THREE

ISLAM'S CLOSE RELATIONSHIP TO TERRORISM

THE FORMAL CHARGE

I am the prosecutor. You, the reader, are the jury. And Islam stands before you on trial for its involvement in the attack against out great nation on Tuesday, September 11th, 2001 - the day that I am calling the Manhattan Massacre. It also stands on trial for being a religion of violence.

I understand that these are serious charges. And, according to logic, when I make a charge I incur the *BURDEN OF PROOF.* Can I prove the charges? Absolutely. I'm getting set to break it down plainly, so you can see the case for yourself!

THE QUR'AN AS THE SOURCE OF THE EVIDENCE

I have no problem in proving my case against Islam. My side is easily proven and my view is rock-solid - though I fully admit that it is not popular right now. Hopefully that will change over time, as people begin to seek out the truth.

I know that within Islam, though the vast majority holds to The Hadith as an authoritative 2nd revelation, there are mixed views of the reliability of some of these texts. So in this book I will stick strictly with the document that no Muslim will argue against - The Qur'an.

For a deeper analysis of Jihad as it appears in The Hadith, log onto the internet and visit www.faithdefenders.com or call 1-800-41TRUTH to order the booklet, "**THE DOCTRINE OF JIHAD ACCORDING TO THE QUR'AN AND THE HADITH**".

SOMETHING TO LOOK FOR GOING FORWARD – MY USE OF COMMENTARY BY ABDULLAH YUSUF ALI

Here on the North American Continent, the most popular commentator amongst all of the Islamic commentators is Abdullah Yusuf Ali. Perhaps Ahmed Deedat is a close 2nd place. But Ali made his own translation of The Qur'an into English, and has lined it extensively with footnotes. Since he is the most popular, I will be quoting his comments extensively to gain insight for you into the Muslim view of certain verses and teachings.

DEFINING THE WORD "JIHAD"

I can cite for you a ton of verses that show the doctrine of jihad in The Qur'an, but this means absolutely nothing unless I first formally define it for you. Why is this necessary? Modern Muslims, in order to make the ancient pagan religion of Islam seem legitimate in today's world, attempt to dress Islam in "nice clothes". It's an evangelism tactic you see all the time in all false religions. What they attempt to do is hide the truth about what Islam actually teaches. And in order to pull this off, they even go so far as to redefine certain Muslim words.

Like I said earlier, this tactic is not unique to Islam. This type of deception is common in all false religious systems. Please don't take my word for it! Do your own research and your own thinking. If you feel led of God to examine comparative religion, what you will begin to see is a pattern unfolding. As you move from one false religion (non-Christian religion or system of though) to the next, you will discover that each of them believes something that is absolutely ridiculous. And their core doctrinal statements and their "scriptures" always refer to it. But in their public presentations of their religion to the press or to potential converts, they take these crazy doctrines and either avoid them altogether or else present them in a different way, "dressed up" to be presentable.

Mormonism, for example, will call Jesus their savior and even make the claim that they are a Christian denomination! But we have to be careful, because they have a different definition for the words "Jesus" and the word "savior" than orthodox Christians.

One can have a conversation with a member of a false (non-Christian) religion and, when they hear that person using the same terminology as their own, they'd think that they both were talking about the same thing as each other. They'd believe that there is not that great of a difference at all between their religions - unless they defined their terms first! Once they heard each other's definitions of the words, they'd see it in a whole different light. They'd realize that their beliefs were actually worlds apart.

Even a member of the Jehovah's Witnesses will say, *"We're Christians"*. The truth is that they're not, but they are masquerading to be used of Satan to fool who they may fool. Their tactic is one of counterfeit. Counterfeit and disguise are the main methods of all false belief systems. Any time you have to lie about something to present a religion, that religion has something to hide. And how contradictory is it to spread something claiming to be a message of truth by the method of speaking lies?!

The modern Muslim movement here in The Americas is using this method and lying to people by toning down its image, and by holding back on telling the truth about what it actually teaches. Westernized Muslim teachers sometimes try to define jihad as, "a spiritual battle" and not a literal one. Sort of an inward struggle of some kind. Or some admit it's a physical battle, but dress it up by saying that it is *"a physical response to a physical attack that someone else has made against the Muslim first"*.

It moves me to laughter to hear some college kid say, *"Islam is a religion of peace. I know because I took this <u>INTRODUCTION TO ISLAM</u> course at the college and, when I asked the Muslim professor if Islam was a religion of violence, he said no".*

Hello? How do you think he is going to answer? Is the teacher voluntarily going to say, *"Okay, I admit it. Terrorism is practiced in Islam, and The Qur'an commands it in order to further the message of Muhammad across the planet."*? Such an honest answer would be refreshing and a nice change of pace, but would both get the professor fired, and generate a lot of bad public relations between the Islamic community and the rest of the country. So for now, they have to keep it quiet and keep up the act to all those who will believe it.

But if I am right, then the real question is: Why would American Muslims distort the facts like that? What are they doing? They're counting on the fact that you, probably having been born and raised right here in America (a Westerner), have no idea about the truth concerning what Islam has always historically believed and taught. Odds are good that you've never even *seen* a Qur'an, much less *actually read* anything in it! They are in a great position. They can pretty much just present to you what Islam is and you, having no frame of reference against which to check their accuracy, have no choice but to accept whatever they say as fact!

The average American citizen has never taken the time to read the Islamic books and things of that nature. So Muslims often get away with passing Islam off as a religion of peace here in America. And we, for the most part, eat the deception up.

So I have felt the need to get a formal definition of "jihad" from a qualified source - apart from the deception that is currently being put out there. Check this out:

> *"Jihad. The duty to fight all unbelievers."*
>
> **ISLAM** by Alfred Guillaume, page 201, Penguin Books, 1954
> *ISBN 014 013 5553*

This is from the glossary of Muslim terms in the back of Guillaume's book, "*Islam*". Notice the definition of the word "*jihad*". It is the duty to fight all unbelievers. Another way it could be worded is *the duty to fight all non-Muslims*.

If you are a Muslim reader, you naturally have 2 questions: Who is Alfred Guillaume and what qualifies him to write about the topic of Islam?

And if you're in the NOI (**N**ation **o**f **I**slam or, as I sometimes refer to it, the **N**ation **o**f **I**gnorance), your real problem with Alfred Guillaume before even opening the book is his name. You probably don't think it is a "Muslim name".

No matter which branch of Islam you come from, these are legitimate questions. Does Alfred Guillaume qualify to write about Islam? See this excerpt from his book and decide for yourself. On the inside cover is a brief bio on him.

> *"Alfred Guillaume was the Head of the Department of the Near and Middle East in the School of Oriental and African Studies, and Professor of Arabic, in the University of London, and later Visiting Professor of Arabic in the University of Princeton, New Jersey. He took up Arabic after studying Theology and Oriental Languages at the University of Oxford. In the First World War he served in France and then in the Arab Bureau in Cairo. He was ordained when he returned to England. He was known in the Islamic world as the editor of THE LEGACY OF ISLAM, which has been translated into several languages, and as the editor and translator of one of the most important Arabic works on philosophical theology. During the Second World War the British Council invited him to accept a visiting professorship at the American University of Beirut where he greatly enlarged his circle of Muslim friends. The Arab Academy of Damascus and the Royal Academy of Baghdad honored him by electing him to their number, and the University of Istanbul chose him as their first foreign lecturer on Christian and Islamic theology. He died in 1965."*
>
> ***ISLAM*** *by Alfred Guillaume, inside cover, Penguin Books, 1954*
> *ISBN 014 013 5553*

Did you just read what that said? Did you recognize those academic institutions? They were the most prestigious. Did you see those subjects he both taught and studied? They're directly related to Islam.   Did you recognize those countries listed in which he is known as a scholar and an authority in Islam? Many of them are Islamic countries with Muslim governments! This man was more than qualified to write his book, and he was certainly qualified to put forth right definitions of words - even a definition of the Arabic word "jihad".

With this in mind, when one looks at the definition of "jihad" that Guillaume has given, it is interesting to note that the phrase *"hostile towards Muslims"* is missing when it is describing the unbelievers that Muslims should be fighting. "Jihad" is not being defined here as the peaceful Muslims responding to those hostile non-Muslims who've first attacked them. But rather, it is a call for all Muslims to fight all non-Muslims.

Guillaume, in my opinion, seems to be pretty friendly towards Islam overall in his book. In my opinion, I think he is way nicer than he should have been. Even still, he honestly cannot get around the right definition of jihad.

But just in case you're not convinced, let us check out a Muslim source. It is Yusuf Ali's footnote # 1270 as he does commentary on Sura 9:20:

"1270. Here is a good description of Jihad. It may require fighting in God's cause, as a form of self-sacrifice. But its essence consists of....an earnest and ceaseless activity, involving the sacrifice (if need be) of life, person, or property, in the service of God."

THE QUR'AN: TEXT, TRANSLATION, AND COMMENTARY by *Abdullah Yusuf Ali, Footnote # 1270, page444, Tahrike Tarsile Qur'an, Inc., 1934 ISBN 094 036 8323*

On that fateful Tuesday morning of September 11th of 2001, the carrying out of jihad did indeed cause the sacrifice of life, people, and property as Ali said jihad may do.

So going forward, whenever I write the word "jihad" I mean: *The duty of all Muslims to fight against and kill any and all people who refuse Islam, even to the point of the*

Brian James Shanley

destruction of life, person, and property in the servitude of the Allah deity of Islam.

NOW THAT WE'VE DEFINED THE TERM, DOES THE QUR'AN ACTUALLY TEACH THIS HORRIBLE DOCTRINE?

Now that we have demythologized the term and given an honest definition of the word "jihad" (and it sounds terrible, doesn't it?), the real question that we need to answer is this: Does The Qur'an teach Muslims to commit acts of jihad?

This is the most important question of all questions involved in this whole controversy. All over the country right now, people are getting on TV and talking about how peaceful, loving, and good Islam is. For that to be true, its "holy" book cannot teach this horribly evil doctrine of fighting and killing anyone who will not convert to Islam.

But on the other hand, if the teaching of jihad, or committing acts of holy war and fighting against the non-Muslims, can be found within the pages of The Qur'an, then we are faced with a different situation. We would then be able to see that the people who are putting forth this innocent version of Islam are greatly deceived. And one would conclude then that Satan has the sentiment of the majority of the people in America right where he wants them, and the environment is perfect for the spreading of this religion. And it is also the perfect setting for the planning of the next attack. Who will be able to detect an enemy they refuse to see?

The question then is simple: Is jihad a Muslim teaching or is it not? There are tons of people running their mouths saying this and that. If you're tired of listening to them, then allow The Qur'an to tell you instead. Keep in mind the definition we have of jihad already, as quoted from scholarly sources. I'll cut to the chase and show you a verse from The Muslim Qur'an that actually contains the word "jihad" in it.

> *"O Prophet! Resort to jihad against the disbelievers and the hypocrites, and be thou harsh with them; their refuge is Gehenna – an evil homecoming!"*
>
> *[SURA 9:73]*

In his book, one of the Muslim authors I've read named Maulana Muhammad Ali writes of this verse:

> *"Here is the Quranic injunction concerning jihad:"*
>
> **MUHAMMAD THE PROPHET**, *by Maulana Muhammad Ali, page 146, Ahmadiyya Anjuman Isha'At Islam LaHore USA, Inc., 1924 ISBN 091 332 1079*

Once again, we see that Muslim scholars back me up in my claims. And I have provided the complete information necessary for you to find the book and look this up for yourself at your leisure, to make sure I am accurately quoting these people. I have even provided the ISBN (International Standard Book Number) to make it easier.

And with the above author, you need the ISBN because when you check into Islamic commentaries, you'll eventually wonder, *"Are there any Muslim commentators who are **not** named Muhammad? Are there any who are **not** named Ali, or any combination of the two?"*. Ha, ha, ha!

But with this ISBN, you can actually pinpoint *which* of the many Muhammads and *which* of the many Alis you are dealing with. Check him out at your local bookstore if you feel the need. He really wrote that. I have been honest and careful in recording his words.

The passage says to "**_Resort to jihad against the disbelievers and hypocrites_**" (non-Muslims). Allah tells Muhammad, the original spreader of Islam, to "**_Be thou harsh with them_**" when dealing with non-Muslims. The acts of holy war committed against non-Muslims by the Muslims are supposed to be of the cruelest nature possible. "**_Their refuge is Gehenna_**" – Gehenna is another word for hell. Islam teaches that there is a hell (like Christianity does, only we are hated because we believe this, yet Islam which teaches the same is celebrated). "**_An evil homecoming_**" – Islam also teaches that Muslims should kill non-Muslims and send us to hell (our home) where we belong.

Knowing what we know about jihad – what it is, what it involves, and what its purpose is – *this passage alone should be enough* to convince you of the truth. It should prove my original charge that Islam is a religion of violence, and even teaches violence to be done by Muslims to non-Muslims.

Therefore it is a reasonable conclusion, if not totally obvious, that Islam played a huge motivational role in the attack against America on September 11th, 2001.

You should be able to understand now that the cries and the urgent pressure by the politicians and the news media about Islam being peaceful are garbage. Their requests to not equate the recent World Trade Center/Pentagon incident of September 11th, 2001 with the religion of Islam are nothing more than a cheap and empty piece of bad information, being forwarded by people who haven't had access to all the facts.

GET OUT YOUR SHOVEL – WE'RE ABOUT TO DIG DEEPER

When you are interpreting literature, context is highly important. So allow me to briefly set up this verse from The Qur'an for you. The unbelievers, or non-Muslims, are in view. Muslims who are reading this passage in The Qur'an are being indoctrinated as to how to view a non-Muslim. Check this out, directly from The Qur'an itself:

> *"They wish that you should disbelieve as they disbelieve, and then you would be equal; therefore take not to yourselves friends of them, until they emigrate in the way of God; then, if they turn their backs, take them, and slay them wherever you find them;"*
>
> *[SURA 4:89]*

Sick, isn't it? If they turn their backs, slay them. Kind of gives new meaning to the phrase, *"He stabbed me in the back"*, doesn't it? This is no joke and not meant to be funny. This is literally written in The Qur'an and I'm quoting it word-for-word!

PEACE NOT AN ISLAMIC OPTION

"If they withdraw not from you, and offer you peace, then restrain their hands, take them, and slay them wherever you come to them; against them We have given you a clear authority."

[SURA 4:91]

Allah here has given the Muslim clear authority, or permission, to do whatever he feels like doing to the non-Muslim. Even if the non-Muslim offers his hand in peace, the Muslim is supposed to kill him anyways.

My question is naturally – what the heck kind of god gives his permission and even commands his followers to do this to other people? Obviously the answer is a wicked, evil, and pagan god.

And my other question is – what kind of a fool gets on the television or the radio and publicly says that a religion which contains such evil as one of its core teachings is actually a religion of peace? Who says that? If they had read this passage, they would never say that.

So obviously the ones who are saying these things have never read this passage before. They are speaking without knowledge. They don't care about truth. They'll make up truth as they go along, and force their made-up truth onto the general public.

I would call this kind of person a misguided, agenda-oriented person who doesn't really care about either learning or spreading the facts. I'm not just talking about

President Bush. It actually seems pretty dominant all over America right now. A sort of make-believe view of reality is being fed by the minority to the majority, and rather than checking into the facts for themselves, this majority is swallowing up wholesale anything the minority says, simply because it was fed to them through TV. A creepy *"don't confuse me with the facts"* mentality is in the air and is the majority view among our citizens. I don't quite understand why our people are refusing to think for themselves right now, but I hope the paradigm shifts as soon as possible.

EITHER CONVERT TO ISLAM AND PAY US MONEY OR WE WILL KILL YOU AND YOUR FAMILY

Before looking at the coming verse, it is important to know that when The Qur'an refers to an "idolater", it refers to a follower of any religion other than Islam. When it refers to "the prayer", it means the prayer that Muslims repeat 5 times daily in submission to their deity, Allah. With these definitions in mind, check out more wisdom from Muhammad:

> *"Then, when the sacred months are drawn away, slay the idolaters wherever you find them, and take them, and confine them, and lie in wait for them at every place of ambush. But if they repent, and perform the prayer, and pay the alms, then let them go their way;"*
>
> *[SURA 9:5]*

Breaking it down into more modern terms, it is saying to Muslims that as long as it is not Ramadan, go ahead with the task of spreading Islam. Anyone who is not already a Muslim needs to either be killed, or converted to Islam and made to pay a fee. Yusuf Ali's footnote # 1251 is helpful in understanding this a little better:

> *"1251. When war becomes inevitable, it must be prosecuted with vigor. According to the English phrase, you cannot fight with kid gloves. The fighting must take the form of slaughter, or capture, or siege, or ambush and other strategems."*
>
> **THE QUR'AN: TEXT, TRANSLATION, AND COMMENTARY,** by Abdullah Yusuf Ali, Footnote # 1251, page 439, Tahrike Tarsile Qur'an, Inc., 1934
> ISBN 094 036 8323

PAY US MONEY, BECOME A MUSLIM, OR DIE – ANOTHER OCCURANCE OF THIS TEACHING

"Fight those who believe not in God and the Last Day and do not forbid what God and His Messenger have forbidden – such men as practice not the religion of truth, being of those who have been given the Book – until they pay the tribute out of hand and have been humbled."

[SURA 9:29]

Let's interpret this verse together to get the meaning out of the text. ***"Fight those who believe not in God"*** – What god is being talked about? Since this is a Muslim writing, we must conclude that the god in view is the Allah deity of Islam. Those who believe not in Allah are non-Muslims. ***"Such men"*** – Men can encompass women and children as well (sometimes we refer to the human race as ***man***kind – we are actually referring to all people in general), and it does here. ***"As practice not the religion of truth"*** – Another reference to non-Muslims. In an Islamic writing, what would be called the religion of truth? Obviously Islam. Those who "practice not" Islam then are, by definition, non-Muslims. They are referred to in 2 different ways as being the people that Muslims should fight and kill. ***"Being of those who have been given the Book"*** – A reference to Jews and/or Christians. And I say "and/or Christians" because Muhammad was not the most consistent fellow I've ever read. In The Qur'an, sometimes the "People of The Book" are the Jews. Other times it is clearly a reference to Christians. And I've even read some Muslim writers who think that the phrase "People of The Book" is supposed to

54

refer to both Jews and Christians at the same time, wherever it is found in The Qur'an. I don't agree with them, but it is another view that exists out there. Of the 3 available options, take your pick.

Because no matter how you slice it, Muhammad clearly wants Muslims to fight and kill a certain group of people ***"until they pay the tribute out of hand and have been humbled"***.

Basically the verse is saying this: *Anyone who will not convert to Islam, especially Jews and Christians, fight and kill them. Or charge them a fee and, when they pay it, you can let them live because their payment is a visible demonstration of which religion is superior – Islam.*

We don't see this happening everyday here in our part of the world, so you may be a little bit surprised to read this. It's not happening here in America – at least not yet. Because Islam is not the dominant religion – yet. And the government is not a Muslim government – and I'm going to again say "yet".

We don't know what is going to happen in the future here in our nation. And judging from the direction things seem headed in currently, the future could go either one way or the other. But clearly, we have just seen yet another passage in the sacred Islamic texts commanding Muslims to commit acts of war against people who don't hold to Islam as their religion.

ALLAH LOVES THE MUSLIMS THAT KILL FOR HIM

It is often said of the god of Islam that when one reads The Qur'an, it is interesting to note that it is nearly impossible to find an account of him being described as a god of love. References to him extending love to his created universe, and even to his own human followers, are extremely rare.

Some wonder if this evil deity loves anyone at all! Well, The Qur'an reveals that there are *some* people that Allah loves. Check this out:

> *"God loves those who fight in His way in ranks, as though they were a building well-compacted."*
>
> **[SURA 61:4]**

So the Allah god of Islam does actually love a group of people! But they are only those who kill in his name. He particularly seems to like it when his people become unified around this killing spree, and look like a well-organized unit when they pull it off.

Does a bunch of guys doing something in harmony, like hijacking 4 planes simultaneously and crashing them one after the other into various targets like clockwork, sound in harmony? Does it sound like they operated like "***a building well-compacted***"? No doubt that those Muslim terrorists had this verse on their minds on that day. It was very well-planned and very organized, just like their god likes it.

They were certainly trying to win their evil god's approval and love.

LIKE IT OR NOT, THE HISTORICAL AS WELL AS THE PRESENT FACTS SPEAK FOR THEMSELVES

If this is your first time reading something like this and you are just shocked so far at how I am painting Islam, I challenge you to do your own study. If you study Islamic history or even world history, you'll quickly catch on to a pattern. You'll see that wherever Islam has been on the face of the earth, wherever it has been in power (through alliances with human government), and wherever it has been the dominant religion, that it has left behind a trail painted red with the blood of innocent people. The governments of those nations, resulting from the leaders being followers of Islam, usually become so corrupt and so blood thirsty that we see the earlier-referenced passages being carried out against the common people over whom they have ruled.

And non-Muslims usually have an ultimatum given to them: *"Either become a Muslim, pay us money, or die"* seems to be the choice they are forced to make.

SMITE THEIR NECKS – STRIKE HOME YOUR BLOWS AT THE NON-MUSLIMS' MOST VITAL POINTS

> *"When you meet the unbelievers, smite their necks, then, when you have made wide slaughter among them, tie fast the bonds;"*
>
> *[SURA 47:4]*

This Sura is named after our boy, Muhammad himself! Woohoo! Anyway, on September 11th, 2001 this verse was obeyed perfectly for the false god Allah by some of his human followers. They ***"made wide slaughter"*** among us here in America, who many Islamic terrorist groups have declared jihad (or holy war) against in years' past. Abdullah Yusuf Ali provides us with an Islamic scholar's interpretation of this passage in his commentary:

> *"Once the fight (Jihad) is entered upon, carry it out with the utmost vigour, and strike home your blows at the most vital points (smite their necks), both literally and figuratively. You cannot wage war with kid gloves."*
>
> **THE QUR'AN: TEXT, TRANSLATION, AND COMMENTARY**, by *Abdullah Yusuf Ali, Footnote # 4820, page 1378, Tahrike Tarsile Qur'an, Inc., 1934*
> *ISBN 094 036 8323*

The first thing that comes to mind when checking out Ali's comments is: Can the man get some new material please? How many times can he repeat the phrase *"You cannot wage war with kid gloves"* in the same book? Ha, ha, ha, ha! I was just kidding!

But seriously, I want you to keep something in mind. That is the most popular commentator here in the West. The American Muslims read him the most. Many of them are studying this verse every day, and other Qur'anic verses just like it. Somewhere right now in your city, just as you sit here and read my book, there is a young Muslim studying The Qur'an's jihad commands. He is learning how to be ready to be called upon by the higher-ups in the structure of the jihad against the Great Satan of The West - code word for the land you love – the home of the free and the brave!

When the call comes in, you'd better believe that this individual, teamed with others, will be hyped up, psyched up, and ready to carry out a holy war and to strike home their blows against all that is non-Muslim, or not submitted to their god, Allah. Since they see us as an infidel nation, and we nationally are not submitted to Allah, then war is declared against us all. They don't care who they take out, as long as those killed are citizens of America. Man, woman, boy, girl, baby, elderly person, physically handicapped person, it doesn't matter. They'd probably be happy to kill your family dog or cat! An American killed is an infidel pig taken off the earth.

In the act of taking out as many of us as possible at one given time, they also want to hit the most vital points of their enemy (America). And for the particular Muslims, some of which are in foreign lands and some of which walk the streets with you and I every day, who've declared this jihad against us, our most vital points were The World Trade Center, The Pentagon, and The White House. The World Trade Center is like a symbol of our economy – our economic strength. The Pentagon was a symbol of our military might. And The White House (thank God they did not get it) is a symbol of our government, which grants the people under it freedom.

It should be beginning to become plainer and easier to see the truth that September 11th, 2001 was the previously-referenced Qur'anic passage, interpreted in the previously-referenced way, by the most popular Muslim American interpreter/commentator that we have, being obeyed and carried out exactly. And it led to the most horrifying loss of life I've ever seen. It's yet another Qur'anic command to commit acts of terror and holy war against others who don't share Islam as their religion.

I keep on quoting these things one after the next so you can see what I have always known to be true, even if it is your first time seeing it in this way.

I must confess that I was once an Islamic sympathizer. I was not happy when confronted with these things that I now write to you. But the facts are the facts, and no honest person can get around them if they're truly seeking to fully understand the Islamic threat for what it really is. In the same way that I had no choice but to alter my view of Islam in order to make it line up with the evidence, so must you. In the same way that when my deep sleep was met with facts, and I had no choice but to wake up, so must you.

I hope you can see the pattern of violence taught in The Qur'an beginning to unfold. The very future of our country is dependent upon our citizens' ability and willingness to wake up and smell the truth.

September 11th, 2001 was Islam in all of its splendor. It was Islam at its finest. It was not a bunch of fanatics or crazies. It was the most common school of thought within Islam, that is the most widely taught all over the world.

ATTENTION ALL AMERICANS: IT IS TIME TO THINK OUTSIDE OF THE COCOON

Some of my friends from other countries tease me about the mentality we have here in our great nation. We at times have what I like to refer to as a "plastic bubble mentality". We see this sort of tunnel vision. If the world were a mile long, we see only a foot of it - only the foot that directly relates to our everyday lives. Only the foot that is right in front of us. Anything outside of the sphere that is our daily life is unimportant to us. We neglect what goes on in other countries because it is outside of our own day-to-day experience in our own country. For the first time, this has now come back to haunt us.

Sometimes we even get to the point where we forget that other countries outside of The United States of America even exist! And to any of my West Coast readers, sometimes you are so inwardly focused that you don't even realize that any place outside of California exists! You at times get so caught up in the goings-on of your state that you think California is the only place there is.

We as Americans have the "plastic bubble mentality", where we live and move and have our being within a fixed sphere. When it comes to world events this truly limits our perspective, and damages our ability to see the big picture.

When you realize that outside of the plastic bubble we live in there exist many other countries, and then look at Islam through worldwide eyes, the view is clearer. My point is easier to see. All around the Islamic world, the way

I am presenting The Qur'an to you is the dominant way of interpreting these verses. I am giving you the majority view that is taught and practiced throughout all of the world of Islam. Who cares what a small amount of them here in America are telling you that Islam teaches? Are we to take what is communicated by a small part of Islam here and apply it to the whole of Islam all around the world? Or does it make more sense to look at the whole of Islam all around the world in order to understand what the small part of Islam here also believes?

Of course the ones over here with us in America are going to say they are peaceful! They're in the minority here. They're trying to assimilate and blend in unnoticed. What would you expect them to say? *"Hello, I'm a terrorist. Your country keeps on getting involved in the Middle Eastern peace process, but is not taking my side. I need to teach your country a lesson. I have this dynamite under my coat. Can I blow you up today?"*

They're not going to make it quite that easy. I'm sorry to disappoint you. They're merely infiltrating our plastic bubble until the appointed time. Then you'll see what happens to us from within. And it will wake you up to the truth about Islam on a worldwide level.

But if you care to, look outside of the bubble. See outside of the cocoon that we live in, and see the grand scheme of things on a worldwide playing field. Name a Muslim country where Islamic terrorism is not existent. Sorry. Time is up. You could not think of one, could you? Wherever you see Islam anywhere (pick a country, any country) you also see terrorism, because Islam and terrorism go hand-in-hand!

I have not misrepresented Islam. This is the historic way that these verses have been viewed for centuries. This is the way these verses are seen in other countries outside of America, by Muslims who are not Westernized and who have no need to pretend that they follow a religion of peace, because they are in the majority over there. You have seen the fruit. My God, brothers and sisters! Open your eyes! We need to stop playing games with our limited scope before it becomes too late!

<u>*DON'T LET OTHER PEOPLE'S OPINIONS OF YOU THROW YOU OFF – DO THE RIGHT THING*</u>

Somewhere right now as you read my book, within our very own borders the next World Trade Center/Pentagon incident is being planned. There obviously is not a World Trade Center to hit anymore, but something of that magnitude is on the horizon. It may even be bigger than the last one.

As you sit here reading, it is being planned out against America at this very hour! And because we're too busy trying to look the other way, and trying to "love one another", we're missing it. The modern diversity movement has us all afraid of our own shadows. Any suspicious activity that we witness, we don't want to report it to the authorities for fear of being called a racist or intolerant by our fellow citizens. The nation-wide "warm fuzzies" that everyone has developed sounds nice and beautiful. But what it has really done is sawed the legs off of our citizens (figuratively), destroyed their right and ability to patrol their own neighborhoods, and has crippled and decreased the intelligence capable of being gathered by our government agencies.

The same people forcing the modern diversity movement onto the masses are going to have the nerve to be upset and shocked when the next terrorist attack comes. They're going to have inter-faith ecumenical gatherings and cry and attempt "to find meaning" as the nation around them crumbles to the ground. They will be unaware of their own contribution to the newest attack.

Forget them. Don't worry what people say about you! You owe it to your God and to your nation to do what is right, no matter what people think of you.

If you are suspicious of something going on in your neighborhood, even the smallest and most seemingly insignificant thing, don't stay quiet. Let someone in authority know immediately, so it can be checked out. As our young people say at a concert, *make some noise*!

If you are wrong, you'll put a few fellow citizens through a small inconvenience, for which you can later apologize. But on the other hand, if you are right, there is no telling how many lives you can save!

Brian James Shanley

THE QUR'AN GIVES US THE RECIPE FOR ALL HELL TO BREAK LOOSE IN THE NAME OF ALLAH

> *"O Prophet, urge on the believers to fight. If there be twenty of you, patient men, they will overcome two hundred; if there be a hundred of you, they will overcome a thousand unbelievers, for they are a people who understand not."*
>
> ## *[SURA 8:65]*

Here we see the command of Islam's god, Allah, to its **_"Prophet"_**, Muhammad. The command is to **_"urge on"_** or encourage **_"the believers"_** or the followers of Islam, the Muslims **_"to fight"_**, or kill. Who are they supposed to kill? Well, at the end of the verse we see the clear answer to that. It's the **_"unbelievers"_**. Who are the unbelievers in a Muslim piece of literature? Non-Muslims! If you are not a Muslim, you are the targeted victim of that command. You are the potential murder victim that the pagan moon deity of Muhammad's Qurayish tribe has commanded Muslims to take out. Pretty sick, huh?

You think that was bad? You haven't seen anything yet! It gets worse. If you stay with the same flow of thought and in the same sura (Sura 8), you eventually run into verse 67:

> *"It is not for any Prophet to have prisoners until he make wide slaughter in the land."*
>
> **[SURA 8:67]**

Consider for a moment exactly where we are at in this analysis. Add both passages together, and you can see the reasoning which provided the psychology necessary in the minds of the September 11th, 2001 terrorists to commit such an act of mass murder.

#1, in verse 65 we saw that The Qur'an gives its readers some kind of weird delusions of invincibility. They are taught that even 20 of them will win out against 200 non-Muslims. Basically summed up, it means that no matter how big of a stunt you're getting set to pull off, no matter how many people or what agencies are opposed to your mission, the Allah god of Islam will help you win out against the *__people who understand not__* – the non-Muslims.

#2, in verse 67 we saw that in a holy war or jihad situation, no prisoners can be taken until first *__wide slaughter__* is made *__in the land__* that the Muslims are trying to conquer.

Add those 2 things up and you have the recipe for all hell to break loose in the name of Allah, and as we have just read, is commanded in The Qur'an. The Muslim terrorist who has these things on his mind has no thought of failure, and no fear of consequences. He or she is eager and excited to carry out any mission for Allah that is commanded by the people in authority in Islam.

COME ON, YOU'RE BEING TOO HARD - ISLAM IS A PEACEFUL RELIGION

The average citizen who is informed about Islam only through the news and TV shows and magazines and other forms of media, or from water cooler conversations in the break room at his/her place of work, yet refuses to pick up the Muslim "scriptures" to find out the truth, is perfectly brain-washed. Whether you talk to one on the East Coast, one on the West Coast, or one somewhere in between, they all sound alike. They've all swallowed the same watered-down version of Islam. They're a dime a dozen and say things like this: *"Islam is a religion of peace. I should know. You see, I saw this on television. There was this speech by this guy and he said so"*.

And I, being the sarcastic funny guy that I can be at times, respond in the most mocking of tones by saying, *"Oh, I see! It was on TV! It must be true! The news media's first priority is to give us, the average citizens, the whole truth. They're totally objective with no hidden motives and agendas. They really believe that we can handle everything, and they spare nothing in getting us the accurate facts. They never lie. I'm so sorry. Please forgive me. I keep forgetting about the absolute reliability and infallibility of the media!"*

This, of course, is just my silly personality making a joke out of their view. Anyone with any sense knows that there is no such thing as an unbiased article or news segment. And anyone who watches the programming being put out about Islam can see that the news networks very much have a view in place, and they're structuring their news stories in a way that has been designed to get their viewers to accept their opinions. One has to be blind, deaf, and dumb to miss it.

So since a news anchor man or news anchor woman probably has a degree in *journalism*, should we accept their views about *religion* too? Or should we be checking out resources put out by people whose area of study is actually religion if we want to know religious truth?

If you needed your tonsils removed, would you go to a dentist for help? No. You'd want the best eyes-ears-nose & throat doctor that you could find. You'd want one who has done this surgery successfully many times before. A dentist, having studied and worked in a total other area, would be considered unqualified to perform such an operation.

A journalist or a politician putting forth ways that people should view religion is the equivalent of practicing tonsil removal with a dental license! It just doesn't work. Mr., Mrs., or Ms. Reader, you don't go to politicians or news broadcasters for religious training and instruction. This is a subject they are unqualified to teach you about. This is an area that is outside of their niche. Do you think you should be accepting whatever they are trying to get you to accept?

Sounds like a no-brainer to me. Too bad so many of us here in America cannot get our minds around so basic of an idea.

DON'T BELIEVE EVERYTHING YOU READ IN THE PAPERS OR SEE AND HEAR ON THE NEWS

I'm encouraging you, my reader, to get with the program. Take off the glasses through which you view life. Clean them, put them back on, and then take another look at the world around you. See things unobstructed and for what they really are. People who put forth the programming on TV have an agenda. It's important to them, in order to achieve certain objectives, that you think a certain way about the social issues of our day. Not just you, but everyone else around you are all targets.

They (the news media) put forth the way people are supposed to view a certain issue or event. They make sure it is so over-exposed that we (the average citizens) all get the point. Sometimes they beat it into the ground so severely that we are sick of hearing about it. But the repetition, no matter how annoying it becomes, usually accomplishes what it has set out to do, and drills into the people how they should think about a certain issue.

Everyone, from the top officer at the university levels down to the kid who enters kindergarten, gets indoctrinated with this view in the educational system. They hear about it so much that they eventually believe it. And they believe it so strongly that they feel that anyone who has not accepted this commonly-believed indoctrination is ignorant. They are seen as behind the times, and not on the cutting edge of the newest trends in modern thought. They are viewed as a cave man or cave woman who must never leave the house, and must not have any access to the outside world, because they have not yet swallowed up what everyone else in our society has been instructed that they are supposed to believe.

Ideas other than the majority view are not tolerated in our society. People who think independently are looked down upon, and their views are called culturally unacceptable, and even dangerous. Try telling someone the truth about Islam and watch them rush to shut you up. When one looks at the opinions of most of our people towards Islam following the attack, it is clear to see that the media has done its job well. The average person is trained perfectly. But I'm asking you not to assume that something is automatically made true just because it is being reported on TV.

DOES ANYONE IN AMERICA TODAY RECALL AN OLD DOCUMENT KNOWN AS THE BILL OF RIGHTS?

Even though the U.S. Constitution says clearly that Congress can make no law respecting an establishment of religion or prohibiting its free exercise, our media and our government are working together to do both to us simultaneously, on the sneak.

They have established a national religion right here in the United States by putting forth the way people should see Islam. By saying that the ones who did the attacks on September 11th, 2001 were not real Muslims, they have set that up as the only way possible one can view that religion. They have closed the door to the idea of any other opinion. The view that Islam is a religion of peace is an established religious worldview that our government is endorsing and actively forcing on everyone!

They have prohibited the free exercise of religion in trying to demonize anyone who dares question the religious view that they have established. If you dare to put forth something other than what is popular, you are suddenly called evil. If you dare to think for yourself and choose to do your own studying and come to your own conclusions, then you had better come to the same conclusion that they have established!

If not, be prepared to be hated and insulted and slandered. This is silly. Our country wants to produce a society full of mindless robots who all think the same way about this event.

I HOPE YOU SEE THE CONTRAST OF METHODS

Unlike the other side of the debate, I'm not quoting you a bunch of empty slogans or catch phrases. I'm not vomiting up the old recycled things I picked up at some ethnic sensitivity class, or some sayings I heard at the diversity seminar. What I'm quoting for you is the *Muslim* scriptures and commentators who are universally recognized by *Muslim* authorities as qualified sources of right information. You have those people and you have me. Which side of the debate puts forth the better case? Who are you going to believe? I don't think the choice is really that difficult. Let us return now to the text of The Qur'an.

Brian James Shanley

ALLAH URGES ON THE MUSLIMS TO BUTCHER ANY OPPONENTS OF ISLAM

In case you are not yet convinced that Islam is a violent religion, check out the next exhibit in my case:

> _"So do thou fight in the way of God; thou art charged only with thyself. And urge on the believers; haply God will restrain the unbelievers' might; God is stronger in might, and more terrible in punishing."_
>
> _[SURA 4:84]_

What this verse says in a nutshell is: _Butcher the opponents of Islam, or those who will not convert to it._ Great religion of peace, isn't it? Aren't you glad people are getting on TV trying to endorse this and keep you from daring to question this kind of stuff?

CONTINUE KILLING UNTIL ALL OTHER RELIGIONS HAVE BEEN WIPED OUT OF THE LAND AND ONLY ISLAM IS LEFT STANDING

> *"Fight them, till there is no persecution and the religion is God's;"*
>
> **[SURA 2:193]**

Here is the breakdown of the passage: ***"Fight them"*** – *Them* contextually is a reference to the unbelievers. Who are unbelievers in Muslim literature? Non-Muslims, of course! Once again, Muslims are told to fight (kill) us. ***"Till there is no persecution"*** – Persecution is referring to other religions. The very existence of another kind of religion on Islamic soil is seen as persecution against Muslims, against Islam, and against Allah. Muslims are to keep on fighting and killing in the land they're trying to conquer until there are no competing religions left in that area. ***"And the religion is God's"*** – Once again I ask you the question: In Islamic literature (like The Qur'an), which god is referred to as *thee* God? The Allah god from Muhammad's tribe. Muslims are to fight and kill through the land until there are no other religions and the only religion left in existence is Allah's - which is Islam (submission to Islam's Allah god).

Bluntly paraphrasing, it says, *"Muslims! Kill all non-Muslims! Or else scare them into submission and conversion by threats of physical violence, until Islam is the dominant religion throughout your land."*

You see, with that kind of mentality there is no freedom of religion permitted. There is not even room for a hint of freedom. Don't take my word for it. Like I always say - do your own digging into the facts and come to it for yourself some day. How many Muslim countries can you name that extend freedom of religion to their citizens? You couldn't name one for sure if your life depended upon it, could you? This is not a coincidence.

YOU CANNOT GO ANYWHERE TO ESCAPE ISLAMIC OPPRESSION

Look at any present-day country in which Islam is the majority religion: Afghanistan, Pakistan, Indonesia, Iraq, Arabia, Lebanon, Iran, etc. Or check out the various African countries through which Islam is spreading like cancer. Ask yourself a question. Don't turn off your brain. Ask yourself hard questions. Be a thinking person. Are any of these nations democracies? Are people born with the right to practice the religion of their choice? Do the people get to vote for the leaders over them? No. Without exception, you'll see nothing but the suppression of basic human rights in any of these places.

And then this forces the question: Why not? It is because freedom of religion and basic human rights are incompatible with Islam. Wherever Islam is the majority religion among the people of a given country, no matter where on the planet you choose to look, what you'll see over and over again without exception is that Islam is forced upon the citizens. No choice is offered. Even a rumor that you might possibly own literature from another religion is a capital crime. If you brought a Bible onto Islamic soil in most of these places all hell would break loose. Why? Because most people in political office in these countries are Muslims. That being the case, they have to obey Qur'anic verses that teach the silencing of religions other than Islam. They have to deal with any hint of going astray from Islam by the people over whom they're governing quickly and severely. They have to squash these things in their infancy, and make an example out of any people who are dumb enough to question Islam, before something other than Islam begins to spread across their land.

YOUR ENEMY IS STILL YOUR ENEMY, WHETHER YOU CHOOSE TO SEE HIM THAT WAY OR NOT

The events described in the last section sound sick, don't they? But do you want to know something even *more* sick? I just watched a cable TV special that tried to paint this religion (Islam) in a peaceful light! They (the producers of the TV show) defended Islam with every breath they had, and with every drop of strength they could muster. It seemed very personal to them for some reason. The producers must have thought they were doing society a favor by running to the defense of Islam.

But do you know what? For any of you readers out there that are defending Islam, you are playing right into the hands of the terrorists. They've won a great victory the minute you start defending Islam. This is exactly how they hope you will think. Both the terrorists in foreign lands and the ones here in America (and yes, there are probably hundreds here right now, walking the streets with you and I every day) love the whole pro-Muslim movement that came out of this whole thing. It falls right into their hands, and sets the perfect environment for them to build for another attack unnoticed. *ANOTHER ONE WILL HAPPEN SOMETIME IN THE NEAR FUTURE.* People are walking around thinking it will not. But you have the book in your hands. I am on record in print telling you it will. Please do not act surprised when it does. You've been given prior notice. September 11th, 2001 was just the beginning.

Perhaps by the time this book has went to print another such horror has happened. I pray every night that I am wrong, but if I am right I will not be surprised.

How many more people have to die in the name of Allah right here in America before our own people take off their blindfolds and see Islam in its true light? Does a weapon of mass destruction have to go off in a major city and kill a couple of million of us before we move?

SHANLEY'S ROBBERY ILLUSTRATION SHOWS HOW VULNERABLE AMERICA REALLY IS

Let me illustrate for you. Suppose you are a robber (no, I'm not condoning criminal activity – this is merely a crude illustration of a point I'm trying to make – stay with me on this). You are dirt poor and you are starving, and you see a rich person coming around the corner. You can tell they have money by how they are dressed. It is night time in a bad neighborhood, yet this person is dumb enough to be walking alone. It seems like a perfectly vulnerable victim. As you approach, you realize they are someone you know. This person knows martial arts and could mess you up badly. But you need the money desperately, so you're going to throw it all on the line and go for it.

They have always known you as a criminal, so if you came looking like you normally look, they would recognize you. You decide to disguise yourself in a Mickey Mouse mask. You approach your intended target and hit him. Even though you are using your trademark style of combat that the whole neighborhood knows about, this person is fooled by your Mickey Mouse mask and does not know it is you. The person, who has a deep arsenal of martial arts moves at his disposal, hears your voice as you demand his money. In the depths of his own heart, he knows it is you behind the mask.

But for reasons that are his own, he chooses not to believe that he is being robbed by you. He believes that Mickey Mouse is standing in front of him, and that both the punch and the voice must have come from some unseen other source. He shuffles to think of a way to identify and respond to this unseen robber. In doing so he leaves himself open to you. You take full advantage and hit him again. He still refuses to recognize that there is a deeper and uglier source of his assault - you. He chooses not to see you beyond the Mickey Mouse mask. In his mind, the person behind the Mickey Mouse mask cannot be robbing him. It's Mickey Mouse for crying out loud! Someone he's always known to be peaceful and good could not be robbing him, right? The robber has got to be someone else. He figures he just has to find out who it really is.

Instead of ripping the mask off of you and then answering your attack with his vast martial arts ability, he looks in a total other direction for the source of the punches that you are throwing at him! It is the dream victim. As a robber, you could not have asked for a better sucker!

What will eventually happen? This person, though he is dozens of times stronger than you could ever be on your best day, will eventually fall because he chooses not to see who is attacking him, nor is he in a position to answer the attack due to his self-imposed blindness. After he falls you will be free to take from him whatever you want, without fear of his dangerous martial arts skills that he has chosen not to use in defense of himself. The only way for him to save himself from getting completely taken out is to choose to actually recognize who's attacking him and then respond with his superior fighting ability. But since he will not, as strong as he is, he is at your mercy.

Now apply that to today. The rich person is America. The robber is orthodox Islam. It is behind the Mickey Mouse mask of the tolerance movement. When orthodox Islam hits us, we refuse to believe that it did. We fail to see the source of the attack. We are looking elsewhere for the real perpetrator. Orthodox Islam stands hidden behind the mask, happy not to be noticed. We are the dream victim.

We are too blind to properly respond to the right attacker. Either we will never respond, we will respond after it is too late, or we can respond now! Choose the 3rd option and respond now! Even if you refuse to see an attacker as your enemy, this does not mean that he still doesn't see you as his enemy!

It is not my intent to seem like a jerk or to come off as mean. I understand the need to be loving to all kinds of people that make up the human race. And I definitely support the freedom of religion that we are currently enjoying here in America (and I say *"that we are currently enjoying"* because there may come a day when this is no longer the case). But at the same time, I don't feel we have to close our eyes and turn off our brains in order to achieve having these things.

BAD RELIGIONS REALLY DO EXIST

Think about it. The ancient pagan religion of witchcraft (which is still around today) that requires the murder of newborn infants only after the kidnapping of them from their parents beforehand - that is evil.

The Hindu gods that require sacrifices and offers of human life - those are wicked.

Whatever religion that Adolf Hitler was following that provided him the theological motivation for his hatred and slaughter of 6 million Jewish men, women, and children - I would suggest that this was vile and disgusting.

So you can see that, contrary to the modern movement of allowing room at the table for every religion, there clearly do exist those religious worldviews for which there should be no room in a civilized society.

And when we look at Islam honestly, in light of its command to go out in the name of its god and slaughter all those who refuse to bow down before him, I would suggest that we're being confronted with a very evil religion. It is comparable to witchcraft, Hitler's anti-Jewish religion, and the religion of the blood thirsty gods of the Hindus. Yes, something that horrifying is in our midst right now. What are we going to do about it?

CRUCIFY, MUTILATE, OR BANISH THOSE WHO RESIST ISLAM

> *"This is the recompense of those who fight against God and His Messenger, and hasten about the earth, to do corruption there: they shall be slaughtered, or crucified, or their hands and feet shall alternately be struck off, or they shall be banished from the land. This is a degradation for them in this world; and in the world to come awaits them a mighty chastisement."*
>
> *[SURA 5:33]*

So for the unbelievers (non-Muslims) or rejectors of Islam, there is a 1-2 punch coming at us. First of all, *in this life* the Muslims that are in power are supposed to do violence to us and kick us out of whatever country we are living in that they would like to occupy. But then, *in the afterlife* awaits an eternal hell.

About this passage I have 2 observations:

#1, yet another card in this stacked deck against Islam which demonstrates from its own sacred writings that it is a religion of violence and terrorism. The Allah deity of Islam commands Muslims to commit acts of violence against non-Muslims. Were the attackers that went out on September 11th, 2001 misunderstanding fanatics? Or were they people who rightly understood exactly what The Qur'an asks them to do, and were they careful about carrying it out?

#2, I'd like to point out interestingly how much Islam is like Christianity in a certain area. It teaches that there is a hell.

CHRISTIANITY AND ISLAM: WHY HATE ONE AND CELEBRATE ANOTHER? EITHER CELEBRATE BOTH OR HATE BOTH. SOCIETY NEEDS TO MAKE UP ITS MIND.

Why did I just bring up the teaching of hell in the previous section? What does it have to do with the book? Well, I'll tell you.

It's all about consistency. The pluralist, tolerant, diversity-loving, multi-culturist society that America has created for herself has major problems. And those problems always result in Christianity being the verbal punching bag of many people.

The people forcing the whole political correctness craze onto everyone else, if they are reading this book, probably think I am more and more bigoted with each Qur'anic verse I cite - as though I wrote The Qur'an or something. These are the silliest people of all.

You see, their whole anti-Christian campaign in the educational institutions, the work place, and the media is fueled by their own personal feelings. They're going to take their own personal opinions and make them the established way of thinking throughout our nation. They hate Christianity and want to teach their hatred of Christianity to the rest of our country.

Their biggest objection to Christianity is the doctrine of eternal torment that is found in The Bible. They criticize, hate, and commit bigotry against Christianity because of their strong emotional rejections of the idea of a hell. How silly is it to commit bigotry in order to spread a message that teaches non-bigotry? This is what the whole diversity movement is doing. In their definition of diversity, there is room for all religions and worldviews at society's table except one - Biblical Christianity!

Another reason Hell probably upsets them is because they think about how unpleasant of an eternity they have to look forward to if they continue on and then die while still in their state of rejection of the truth of Christianity. This alone could be a major cause of their rebellion and antagonism against us.

People like this spend every minute of every day trying to suppress the truth from coming to their minds and attempt to block out any thoughts of hell. Whenever it is mentioned in their presence, it triggers images of torment in their minds and then they have to begin the process of suppression and blocking it out all over again. This angers them and they immediately take it out on the person who brought it up (a Christian) and the belief system that teaches it (Christianity).

Hell does not exactly tickle the human ear. I readily admit it. Perhaps if I had written The Bible I would not have included it. But, like it or not, it is there! And since Christian theology and practice is based upon The Bible, Christianity teaches about it.

There is also another reason why Christianity is on the receiving end of such harsh treatment. People hate Christianity because of its exclusivist nature. When a religion is an exclusivist religion, it teaches that only *its followers* will go to heaven and no one else. This is an anti-establishment view because universalism and ecumenism are trendy right now in our culture. Our public school system is training up a whole generation of universalists and ecumenicists as we speak. They are being taught to think and talk like this:

"If the God of Christianity is really a loving God, He would never send anyone to hell. The fact that Christians talk about heaven as though it is some exclusive supper club or a members-only establishment is upsetting to me. How intolerant! Why only let Christians in but nobody else? Why not allow everyone else in too? Do you mean to tell me that an essentially good Being would damn someone to hell just because they don't believe a certain way? Why make people suffer and go to hell simply because they are not a Christian? This is religious discrimination. Since He discriminates, the Christian God is a bigot. And I refuse to believe in or worship a Great Bigot in the sky."

Dealing with people who have been programmed with this mentality can be both humorous and irritating at the same time. Sometimes when talking to one I seriously wonder if they've ever thought an independent thought in their whole life, or if they have just swallowed everything that has ever been fed to them by our culture without examining it.

Based on the fact that the unbelievers' eternity as described in The Bible doesn't fit into the box that is the person's brain, this person will reject and even talk trash about Christianity.

This person wants reality in the afterlife to conform to their preconceived ideas of what they imagine the afterlife should to be like! Amazing.

I have no problem with the average person in our culture voicing their opinions. I have no problem with them believing what they want to believe, even if I disagree with it. This freedom is what makes our nation great!

The problem I have, though, with people of that mindset is this: If they hate Christianity because of *its* hell, then why are they on TV defending Islam and *its* hell? Why are they so inconsistent?

In addition to the existence of hell, Islam also teaches exclusivism when it teaches that all non-Muslims are going to hell. The residents of hell, according to The Qur'an, will even include the news media people and government employees who are defending Islam! This is according to its own "scriptures", which I have just quoted for you earlier! Re-read it again if you don't believe me!

The tolerance and diversity promoters need to wake up. They need to fine-tune the problems in their program that they are forcing onto everyone all over our country. It is doing more damage than good. It is a logically and philosophically flawed system of thought, as well as an empty approach to life.

The point of this section of the book is that Islam teaches to kill unbelievers (non-Muslims) and send them to hell. For any of you out there who are diving to the aide of Islam in an attempt to save its image in the public eye, you need to understand that in doing so ***you are defending an exclusivist religion***. You need to understand that ***you are defending the doctrine of hell***. These are two teachings for which the world hates Christianity! How can they honestly rally around Islam which teaches these same things?

When any of you defend Islam so passionately, which also teaches the things that are reasons for your hatred of Christianity, you are making a mistake. In the depths of your own conscience, even you know that I am right about this issue.

Anyone who is trying to pass Islam off as peaceful is really embarrassing themselves in a very public way in the eyes of anyone who knows about the Qur'anic verses that I am citing.

As a whole, we here in America have got to wake up! We've got to re-examine our views of Islam in light of the actual facts. We cannot let what is trendy and popular in American thought for a short time period blind our eyes.

If you're going to hate *one religion* for its belief in the doctrine of hell, then be consistent and hate *all religions* who believe in a doctrine of hell.

If you're going to give *one religion* a hard time because it's an exclusivist religion which teaches that only its members will go to heaven, this is fine. Go ahead and give them a hard time. Just be sure to carry out your bigotry to its logical end and give *all exclusivist religions* an equal hard time.

But they will not. They will pick and choose which religion to mess with (Christianity) and which one to leave alone (Islam). This is the greatest deficiency of the modern diversity movement's whole social agenda. The people putting it out there have no problem by-passing one religion that teaches things they don't like in order to lift up, put onto a pedestal, and even celebrate another religion who also teaches the same things they don't like. In my view, I would suggest that such people are guilty of the very prejudice and discrimination that their movement claims to be opposed to. Such a contradictory philosophy is full of holes and hypocritical, to say the least. It is also unlivable. In order to make it consistent, they'd have to equally hate Islam with as much anger as they hate Christianity. But they're too busy teaching cultural awareness curriculums that are teaching people to love Islam.

The minute one comes to the defense of Islam in the name of "diversity" and "cultural awareness" and every other thing that they think is good, they've just contradicted all that their movement stands for. It is a contradiction because they would never come to Christianity's defense like that - and due to what it teaches, even though Islam teaches the same two things which they hate. They're actually showing favoritism and religious bias, which their whole movement claims to be against!!

So next time you meet a hyper-liberal who is defending Islam with more passion than he'd defend his own mother with, remind him that Islam teaches that only Muslims go to heaven (exclusivism), and that all non-Muslims go to hell (the doctrine of eternal torment). Then ask him to either hate Islam just as fiercely as he hates Christianity, or else ask him to renounce his hatred of Christianity altogether! When he refuses to do either one or the other, then you will be able to see that he is not interested in being unbiased, but instead is anti-Christian to the core!

MAKING WAR AGAINST NON-MUSLIMS IS ONE OF THE PRIMARY DOCTRINES OF ISLAM

When you have an unintelligent religion that cannot be spread through great preaching to or by logically reasoning with potential converts, your only other alternatives are to either watch it die out or spread it by the sword. Islam has historically done the 2nd of the 2 choices and carried it militarily across the world, slaughtering those who would not submit to Arabia and Arabia's deity, Al-Ilah. They've used this method because The Qur'an tells them to do it that way.

Islam is a violent religion. If you only remember one sentence from this entire book, remember that one. Islam is a violent religion.

In spite of the verses that I am showing you, there are still those poor and ignorant souls running around our very own country saying that Islam doesn't teach violence! I can remember a time in my life earlier on when I thought I was a citizen of a land that values education! Man, was I off!

People measure your level of intelligence nowadays based solely upon how "in agreement" you are with the way of seeing the world that is fed to you by those above you. If you have totally swallowed up what is taught in public schools and other places, then you are seen as tolerant and virtuous. You are culturally aware. You are hip and on the cutting edge. You are seen as understanding of the times. The less questions you have of the whole movement, and the more of its catch-phrases that have become a part of your everyday speech with other people, the more you are respected in our society.

This is not education. This is indoctrination. There is no better way to control the masses than to teach them what to think, and then make sure that they are all thinking it. If you are an independent thinker, you are suddenly seen as ignorant and even dangerous because you do not share the opinion that everyone else does. But this is not right at all, is it?

Exercise your God-given freedom to think for yourself as we move on in this book. Hopefully you will see what I am talking about. Hopefully it is already starting to click for you, and you are beginning to understand what we are dealing with when we deal with Islam.

In the next area of the book, we'll look at another call to violence that Muhammad once preached, and that Muslims must still obey to this day.

As I am giving you more and more Qur'anic verses, I hope you can see that there is not just one obscure verse I am referring to and depending upon to make my case. But, much the opposite, the flow of the whole Qur'an teaches Muslims to make war against non-Muslims until Islam is the majority religion everywhere - all over the planet. When you go on after this book to do your own research, your own thinking, and your own reading, you will come to this conclusion for yourself (if you are at all honest in your interpretation of the available evidence).

KILLING IN THE NAME OF ALLAH IS COMMANDED BY HIM AND HE CALLS IT A GOOD THING

> *"Prescribed for you is fighting, though it be hateful to you. Yet it may happen that you will hate a thing which is better for you; and it may happen that you will love a thing which is worse for you; God knows, and you know not."*
>
> ## *[SURA 2:216]*

Let's interpret together and get the meaning out of this verse. ***"Prescribed for you is fighting"*** – The Muslim reading this passage can clearly see that he or she has been predestined or ordained to fight (kill) in the name of Allah. ***"though it be hateful to you"*** – Even if that person is having a conscience issue about committing murder, or for some other reason does not want to participate, they have no choice. Allah has ordered them to carry this out. ***"Yet it may happen that you will hate a thing which is better for you; and it may happen that you will love a thing which is worse for you; God knows, and you know not."*** – Man is sometimes blind to what is best for him or her. Though they don't understand why they're supposed to do it, or possibly even reject or dispute the teaching of this prescribed killing, they have no choice but to obey the deity of Islam's divine command.

It seems to be based upon the understanding that Allah knows what is best for the Muslim, though the human individual to whom the command is given cannot see it at that time. Killing non-Muslims is good for them, whether they understand it or not. Kind of like when you were a kid. Your mom made you eat vegetables when you didn't want to because they were good for you. Even if you don't want to kill anybody, Allah makes you do it anyway because it is good for you.

There you have it, yet another reference to the prescribed or commanded fighting and killing that Muslims must carry out if they are seeking to practice Islam correctly. Muslims have to kill or force conversions onto non-Muslims wherever and whenever they come across them. Once again, please do not take my word for it. I am not a Muslim. Let us look to a Muslim scholar to shed some light onto the issue for us to get the classic Islamic interpretation of this passage.

Am I some evil angry Christian who has a deep anti-Islamic axe to grind? Am I twisting the meaning of the Qur'anic text? Well, in Abdullah Yusuf Ali's commentary, you'll find that the most popular Muslim commentator on the North American continent agrees with me. So if I have an anti-Islamic axe to grind, then so does he. If I'm misinterpreting the text, then so is he.

> *"236. To fight in the cause of Truth is one of the highest forms of charity. What can you offer that is more precious than your own life?"*
>
> **THE QUR'AN: TEXT, TRANSLATION, AND COMMENTARY**, *by Abdullah Yusuf Ali, Footnote # 236, page 84, Tahrike Tarsile Qur'an, Inc., 1934*
> *ISBN 094 036 8323*

In that same footnote Ali went on to add more information:

> *"If you offer your life to the righteous Imam, who is only guided by God, you are an unselfish hero."*
>
> **THE QUR'AN: TEXT, TRANSLATION, AND COMMENTARY**, *by Abdullah Yusuf Ali, Footnote # 236, page 84, Tahrike Tarsile Qur'an, Inc., 1934*
> *ISBN 094 036 8323*

You see that? Even the most popular Muslim commentary used here in the West agrees with this Christian. In Islamic Studies this verse is seen as a reference to killing in the name of Allah being ordained or commanded. And it is agreed upon that this killing, especially if it costs you your own life, is seen as a good thing by Allah. Could it possibly get any worse? I'm afraid so. Read on.

SPREAD ISLAM EVERYWHERE AND KILL ANYONE WHO WILL NOT SUBMIT TO ALLAH – HEAVEN AWAITS AS YOUR REWARD

"God has bought from the believers their selves and their possessions against the gift of Paradise; they fight in the way of God; they kill, and are killed; that is a promise binding upon God in the Torah, and the Gospel, and the Koran; and who fulfills his covenant truer than God?"

[SURA 9:111]

Did you read that? ***"God has bought from the believers"*** – In an Islamic piece of literature (The Qur'an definitely is a piece of *something!*), the believers would be followers of Islam; Muslims. Notice that he does not say *"God has bought from the Osama Bin Laden's terrorist group"*. He does not say *"God has bought from the Hamas terrorist group"*. He says he has bought from the *believers*. Whatever he's about to say is universal in scope, and refers to all Muslims. ***"their selves and their possessions against the gift of Paradise;"*** - Allah has given the Muslims the promise of heaven in exchange for the surrender, or giving up, of the things of this world. This could be a reference to a getting rid of earthly material things. But the context also seems like it could refer to being separated from their earthly lives by being killed. Whatever this surrender of their selves and their possessions involves is about to be explained in greater detail. ***"they fight in the way of God;"*** – And once again, in Islamic literature, God is defined as the Allah deity of Muhammad's tribe. ***"they kill, and are killed;"*** – Part of the mission to heaven for the Muslim involves killing other people, and possibly even

99

surrendering their own lives for the cause of advancing Islam. ***"that is a promise binding upon God in the Torah, and the Gospel,"*** - What qualifies Muhammad to comment on either two? The genius could not even read! His constant mistakes about the contents of The Bible and the beliefs of Christianity and Judaism are forever preserved as evidence that God had nothing to do with authorship of The Qur'an. ***"and the Koran"*** – Don't be shocked. Even Muhammad says that going to paradise in exchange for slitting some throats is a promise binding upon Allah in The Qur'an.

I can imagine what some people must be thinking at this point. Probably something like this: *"The what? A promise binding upon Allah in the Koran (another way to spell Qur'an)? It can't be! You see, the people on TV say that the Qur'an doesn't teach such things. Even my Muslim teacher at the university said the same thing. Why would he lie? Say it ain't so."*

I wish I could say it isn't so, but then I'd be just as dishonest as they are. My love for the truth and my love for this country prevent me from caving in to social movements, no matter how popular they are, or how powerful of an influence they wield. As I've just quoted from the records of the speeches of the founder of the religion himself (Muhammad), it is obvious that orthodox Islam teaches that this kind of killing is a part of Islamic practice. Another brick in my case.

ALLAH WANTS TO TERRORIZE NON-MUSLIMS INTO CONVERSION, SO MUSLIMS ARE TO STAB US IN THE THROAT AND CHOP OFF OUR FINGERS

> *"I shall cast into the unbelievers' hearts terror; so smite above the necks, and smite every finger of them!"*
>
> **[SURA 8:12]**

Contextually, this is the god of Islam speaking. These are the words of Allah. Read it for yourself sometime if you do not believe me.

The unbelievers to whom he is referring are non-Muslims. This god, Allah, wants to instill terror into the hearts of non-Muslims. How does he want to scare us? I say "us" because I am not a Muslim. Are you a Muslim? If not, then you had better pay attention, because those who are Muslims and who read this verse are being trained as to how to deal with you. This is what Allah wants done to you according to this passage – unless either Muhammad wrongly spoke it or unless the scribes wrongly recorded what he has said. But like it or not, the verse is there.

Allah wants his human followers, the Muslims, to smite us. He has even specified that we are to be hit with the sword right above our necks. This is probably a reference to going either for the throat or the jugular vein. No matter which way it is interpreted of those two options, it is still quite a violent picture being painted, isn't it?

101

In addition, Muslims have herein been commanded to chop off our fingers as well. In most Islamic countries where the government uses Islamic principles as their rules of the land, these verses are used and carried out exactly, down to the very body parts that they cut off! They will defend themselves and say that they only do this to criminals. But it is worth noting that in those very same countries, a citizen is prosecuted as a criminal who believes in or practices a religion other than Islam!

People who are not in the government but are seeking to follow Islam still need to follow this verse and others like it. If they failed to, then they would cease being Muslims in the right sense of the word.

While the average citizen who follows Islam has no ability to bring someone up on charges and have a trial because they are not the government, they have still found ways to carry out the principle behind this verse.

Some branches of Islam do not see this verse as literal. They still want to be used of Allah to instill terror or fear into the hearts of other Muslims, but will do it by any means necessary. It may not literally be chopping off fingers. It may not be literally slitting throats or smiting above necks. It may be something different - like crashing planes into sky scrapers that are located in non-Muslim nations. Or like blowing up government buildings. Some Muslim groups think this way is better because of the numbers of people that can be taken in one shot.

So while Muslims may not be unified in *how* they kill unbelievers, they all are unified in the belief that *they must*.

It's in The Qur'an and they cannot get around it. And if you, my reader, are seeking to gain a real understanding of September 11th, 2001, then you cannot get around it either.

You may think I am being difficult or harsh, but rest assured I am not alone in my interpretation of this Qur'anic verse as a literal war passage:

"1189. The vulnerable parts of an armed man are above the neck. A blow on the neck, face, or head, finishes him off. If he has armour it is difficult to get at his heart. But if his hands are put out of action, he is unable to wield his sword or lance or other weapon, and easily becomes a prisoner."

THE QUR'AN: TEXT, TRANSLATION, AND COMMENTARY, *by Abdullah Yusuf Ali, Footnote 1189, page 418, Tahrike Tarsile Qur'an, Inc., 1934 ISBN 094 036 8323*

One can argue with *me* all they would like. But are they willing to argue with the most popular commentator that is being read by the American Muslims today?

Ali is like me in saying that the principles described, being the words of Allah, are about physical combat. So much for the liberal Muslim position that jihad is a spiritual or inward battle!

The principles communicated in the Qur'anic verse I have cited are not just for one sect of Islam. They are to all Muslims. They are to be applied by all Muslims in all time periods, all countries, all cultures, and all locations. Yes, this includes right here in America.

Are you still not convinced that Islam is an evil religion? Are you still doubting that the Allah god of Islam is an evil, violent, and pagan deity? Well, read on.

ALLAH IS A MURDERER - AND HIS MUSLIMS ARE HIS WEAPONS THROUGH WHICH HE KILLS

If you keep on reading down in the same sura (8), you will realize that it continues the same flow of thought as the above verse. Eventually you will hit verse 17.

> *"You did not slay them, but God slew them;"*
>
> **[SURA 8:17]**

Think about this for a second. Back in the previous section we looked at verse 12. Allah wanted to put terror into the hearts of the non-Muslims through his human instruments, who are the Muslims. He wanted to do this by smiting the non-Muslims above their necks and chopping off the non-Muslims' fingers.

But now as the idea is developed further, a few sentences later it gets even uglier. According to this verse (17), even though the Muslims are the ones who are carrying out the killing, the one who is actually slaying (killing) them is Allah himself! I don't care who you are, in your heart you know that this is wicked as hell.

Allah wants to force people to submit to him, or accept Islam, by killing all who will not. And his followers, the Muslims, are the chosen vessels through whom he wants to accomplish this horror. Allah is the all-mighty puppeteer, and the Muslims are simply the puppets that he guides to carry out his will in the sick puppet show called human life, on this stage called the earth. When he guides one of his puppets to act out what he is trying to achieve, he has let us know that it is not the Muslim puppet that is responsible for the carnage, but the puppet master himself, Allah, is the real murderer behind it all.

I know it is horrible, but everyone on TV and radio right now is defending this religion.

CONVERT OR WE WILL KILL YOU, ROB YOUR DEAD BODY, AND THEN USE THE MONEY IN YOUR POCKETS TO FUND THE SPREAD OF ISLAM

> *"Say to the unbelievers, if they give over He will forgive them what is past; but if they return, the wont of the ancients is already gone!"*
>
> **[SURA 8:38]**

"*Say to the unbelievers*" – Unbelievers are non-Muslims. Muslims who study this verse are being taught what to say to them. **"*If they give over He will forgive them what is past;*"** – If the non-Muslim will convert to Islam, Allah will forgive them for all of the time in the preceding years of their life where they were not a Muslim. **"*But if they return*"** – If they turn away from the offer of Islam, **"*the wont of the ancients is already gone!*"** – The same things should be done to them that have been done to rejectors of Islam in times' past.

The next verse goes on to say:

> *"Fight them, till there is no persecution and the religion is God's entirely; then if they give over, surely God sees the things they do;"*
>
> *[SURA 8:39]*

"*Fight*" – Or kill. **"*them*"** – The non-Muslims. **"*till there is no persecution*"** – Or competing religious worldviews. Muslims countries always see the spreading of anything other than Islam in their country as a kind of persecution against Islam. **"*and the religion is God's*"**

entirely;" – Until Islam is the dominant religion across the land. *"then if they give over"* – If they convert to Islam by submitting to the pagan moon idol named Al-Ilah, *"surely God sees the things they do;"* and will reward them for coming over to the "truth" of Islam.

If they receive an answer in the negative and a person will not convert to Islam, they are to kill that person. After that person is dead, they are supposed to go through that person's pockets to see if they had any money on them at the time of their death. If so, it is to be taken from him or her and used to continue on the path of blood to convert the world to Islam.

> *"Know that, whatever booty you take, the fifth of it is God's, and the Messenger's,"*
>
> *[SURA 8:41]*

It says that 1/5 is supposed to go to "the messenger" because it was something Muhammad spoke about and did while he was alive. How do you think the early Muslims financed themselves? This was before any oil had been discovered in that part of the world. They robbed and looted whoever would not become a Muslim!

Does The Qur'an leave room open for this to be practiced in today's world? Well, Ali seems to think so.

> *"1209. The rule is that a fifth share is set apart for the Imam (the commander) and the rest is divided among the forces."*
>
> **THE QUR'AN: TEXT, TRANSLATION, AND COMMENTARY,** *by Abdullah Yusuf Ali, Footnote # 1209, page 425, Tahrike Tarsile Qur'an, Inc., 1934*
> *ISBN 094 036 8323*

Since there is not a "prophet" Muhammad to give 1/5 to, you instead give the 1/5 to whoever is leading your band of soldiers on the killing spree. Notice that all of Ali's verbs are present tense. This act (killing those who will not convert and then robbing their dead bodies in order to finance the spreading of Islam) is not some remote ancient practice. It still applies today!

ONCE YOU ARE WELL-PREPARED TO CARRY IT OUT, THEN YOU MUST GO AHEAD IN THE NAME OF ALLAH AND TERRORIZE ANY AND ALL NON-MUSLIMS

> *"Make ready for them whatever force and strings of horses you can, to terrify thereby the enemy of God and your enemy, and others besides them that you know not; God knows them. And whatsoever you expend in the way of God shall be repaid you in full; you will not be wronged."*
>
> *[SURA 8:60]*

"Make ready for them" – *"Them"* is the non-Muslims, according to the context of this sura. ***"whatever force"*** – Any weapon or anything that can be used as a weapon against the non-Muslim is fine. Airplanes are not excluded in this verse. Room is left open for them and worse. The idea is to prepare whatever you can get and be ready to go out for the great cause of advancing Islam. ***"and strings of horses you can,"*** – At the time this was originally "revealed" and even today in some Muslim countries, horses and other animals are used as transportation. Same idea; *Get whatever you can and be ready to use it* ***"to terrify thereby the enemy of God"*** – "Enemy of God" is a reference to non-Muslims. I can say this from life experience as I have been called an enemy of God by more than one Muslim, from more than one different country, because I was unwilling to renounce Christianity and become a Muslim. On one internet web site, "enemy of God" became a nick name used by Muslims to refer to me for a while! ***"and your enemy,"*** – Any enemy of Allah's is supposed to be thought of by his human followers (Muslims) as an enemy of their own. *"and others besides them that you know not; God knows them."* When you go out in the name of Allah to kill some of his enemies of which you are aware, there exists a possibility that he'll also use you to hit one of his enemies of which you are unaware! Nice little bonus, huh? Pretty sick, if you ask me. *"And whatsoever you expend in the way of God"* – Interesting to note that killing non-Muslims is called "the way of God", isn't it? Are any of you who don't think Islam was involved in the attack against America paying attention? *"shall be repaid to you in full;"* – For what the Muslim loses on this side of the grave in this killing he or she will be rewarded on the other side of the grave in Allah's heaven. *"you will not be wronged."* – The idea is that the stunt that you're getting set to do in the name of Allah will go smoothly, and will not fail no matter what. Another illusion of invincibility offered to the Muslim who decides to do this for Allah. Imagine the great psychological condition created by this belief!

The Muslim terrorist who studies this verse right before hijacking a plane has these inspirational words ringing in his head throughout that day, giving him the motivation to do what he has to do for Allah, fully believing that he will be unstoppable. What human being or what human agency can prevent the will of God from happening? Since this person believes that he is actually doing God's will, he is energized and psyched up to get the job done. No fear of failure enters their mind. No feelings about potential consequences enters their heart. Nothing will sway him from his desire to carry it out. Disaster is always the result.

LET US KILL IN THE NAME OF ALLAH – IF WE DIE WHILE DOING IT, WE GET TO GO TO HEAVEN

"So let them fight in the way of God who sell the present life for the world to come; and whosoever fights in the way of God and is slain, or conquers, We shall bring him a mighty wage."

[SURA 4:74]

Those ***"who sell the present life for the world to come"*** are Muslims. The verse says to ***"let them fight in the way of God"***. It could also rightly be translated as "let them kill for Allah". Any Muslim who obeys this verse and becomes a casualty is promised entrance into the Muslim heaven once again. This promise of heaven is more than likely what the phrase ***"We shall bring him a mighty wage"*** is referring to.

ANYONE WHO IS NOT A MUSLIM IS NOT ONLY AN ENEMY OF ALLAH AND THE MUSLIMS, BUT IS A FRIEND OF THE DEVIL TOO

> *"The believers fight in the way of God, and the unbelievers fight in the idols' way. Fight you therefore against the friends of Satan; surely the guile of Satan is ever feeble."*
>
> *[SURA 4:76]*

"Believers", or Muslims, fight in the way of Allah. It means they kill for Allah's cause, which is the advancement of the religious idea of submission to him (Islam) by everyone on earth. **_"The unbelievers"_** and **_"the friends of Satan"_** are the non-Muslims. Muslims are supposed to fight against and kill them whenever and however they can.

BACK TO THE ORIGINAL CHARGES

Do you remember reading the early part of this chapter of the book? My original charges against Islam still remain. I still charge Islam with being a violent religion, and commanding its believers to commit acts of violence against people of other religious views. And I charge it with having been the motivational factor which guided along the September 11th, 2001 attack against America.

I've put forth my proof. What did you think of it?

By reading this book, you have not been given a thorough or scholarly look at violence and its relationship to Islam. You've merely been given a brief introduction at best. Much more could be said about it. I could write a ton more and blast you with so much information that you'd probably be stuck looking at a book several inches thick! But this is not necessary.

I hope, at least, that you have seen my point. I hope that you've been informed that, even though everywhere you look you see someone telling you that Islam is peaceful, another view exists out there in the world. I hope you have even been convinced that this other view that exists is the real truth. And I hope that you will conform your view of Islam to match this truthful view. And then I hope you will communicate your new view of Islam with your family and friends.

I am able to cite the Muslim "scriptures" from The Qur'an that come out and teach Muslims to kill non-

Muslims for the great cause of advancing Islam across the earth.

The people on TV who want you to see Islam as peaceful can quote nothing from The Qur'an to defend their position. They just say it and move on in their presentation, not bothering to prove their statement. To them, they have a cultural movement to advance and they will advance it no matter what the contradicting facts say. I hope now that you can see through what they are attempting to feed you.

Society's current diversity craze, though it might mean well, actually suppresses freedom because it does not allow anyone to hold to an opinion outside of the box that the movement has created. There is an established way you are supposed to think. Anyone who dares even to *hint* like they may be thinking outside of the box is labeled as "ignorant", "bigoted", and even "dangerous". We cannot allow this movement to suffocate our minds or we will miss out on the truth about Islam. And we will be left wondering what happened the next time America gets hit.

If you only remember one thing from this book, remember this: Islam is a violent religion. And its brainwashed followers are the ones who attacked us on September 11th, 2001. And they will attack our country again.

THE BOOK CONCLUDES: AUTHOR'S CLOSING REMARKS

I hope you can see, and agree now that Islam is a violent religion. I hope you can see that it didn't possibly play some *minor role* behind the attacks of September 11th, 2001. In contrast, it played *the lead role*.

Just as disgusting as the act of terrorism itself was, even more disgusting is how we've all reacted to it. The claim these days is that these attacks were some isolated incident not done by real Muslims, but rather a group of crazy nuts and fanatics. People seriously believe that all we have to do is find one small group of problem people, wipe them out, and everything will be fine. If only it were that simple! We are not dealing with a small group of problem people. We're dealing with a religion that is hostile towards anything or anyone that is not like it. It is hostile towards America. It will stop at nothing until it makes America crumble. And it just happens to be the fastest-growing religion on our streets!

The teaching going around out there now is that Islam doesn't teach people to commit acts of violence against non-Muslims or anyone else.

But in this book, we've just examined The Qur'an and found a ton of instances where this *is* taught. And I honestly believe that in this study we did not even break the surface of the acts of violence that The Qur'an teaches Muslims to perform. I could have easily went on for 75-100 more pages.

And when you conclude that The Qur'an is the book which serves as the sacred scriptural text upon which Islamic theology and practice is built, then you have no other choice after this examination of Islam that we have just done. You are in a position in which you are forced to conclude that, contrary to the majority of people out there on television these days, that violence is actually taught in Islam. And the sad and scary thing is that yes, it will more than likely happen again.

To say that the media is right just because the majority of Americans have swallowed the view that it's trying to feed them is a logical error. The error (also called a fallacy) is called *argumentum ad populum*. Ad populum arguments are bad because they assume that something is made true or false based solely upon how many people believe it. This means that if some new philosophy or belief comes out onto the scene, all it has to do is catch on with the majority of the people and it is automatically and magically made true.

Allow me to illustrate. If all of the neighbors on your block one day suddenly decided that the moon was made out of cheese, would this magically change the elements that make up the moon rocks into the same elements that make up cheese? Would everything about the moon suddenly change due to the fact that the people on your block believe something different about it than they previously did? Absolutely not. Because determining what the moon is made out of cannot be based on how the majority of people see it. It has to be based upon evidence. As a simple point of logic, a misguided majority could corporately adopt a view of something that is way off base. And a small minority of people who have actually studied an issue for themselves, apart from the misguided majority, could be right about it. It is possible. It could happen.

Apply this same law of logic to Islam. Just because the liberal, agenda-oriented media has the minds of the majority of our people believing that Islam is a peaceful religion, does this magically make the verses I've quoted to you in this book disappear from copies of The Qur'an all over the world?

Does the fact that the majority believes that Islam is a religion of peace somehow erase the commentators' works that I've quoted which back up my interpretation of The Qur'an?

Does it suddenly clean up and fix the oppression taking place under Islamic rule in many countries around the world? Does it re-write the history of Islam and the death and destruction it has brought to the world? No.

As with my moon illustration above, it's not *the opinion of the majority of the population* that determines truth. It's *the evidence.*

To say that the liberal view of Islam is the correct view of Islam, based upon the fact that it is the position held by the majority of the people in America, is to allow other people to think for you! The majority probably doesn't actually feel that way deep down inside of their hearts, anyways. They are only following what the people over them have told them, and have trusted those people to be honest.

We cannot afford to blindly follow what other people have tried to make us think about Islam and about September 11th, 2001. Some people like that approach because then they are not responsible to do the necessary reading and thinking that is needed to form an informed, educated view of this topic. But if you are not like that, then you should hold to a view not because everyone else buys it, but because you have studied and have thought through it.

If the majority says that Islam is non-violent, yet a minority can demonstrate from *Muslim writings* that the majority is wrong, then one who holds to the majority view would need to either ignore facts and keep right on believing what he believes, or change his view.

My readers, the majority once thought that the earth was flat. The majority was wrong.

The majority once thought that slavery was right. The majority was wrong.

Today the majority thinks that real and true Islam had nothing to do with the September 11th, 2001 attacks against America. Today the majority is dead wrong. I've just demonstrated that to you.

As I close out this 3rd and final chapter of this book, let me just ask to think it all over. Think back to the beginning of this chapter. Remember my charges against Islam and its teachings of violence and its role in the September 11th, 2001 attacks against our nation. Then consider each of the bricks in this case I have laid out before you. It is a rock-solid wall that has been built for my view that yes, Islam teaches Muslims to commit acts of murder and war.

This being the case, I submit to you that Islam, Allah, Muhammad, and The Qur'an all motivated the terrorist attacks of September 11th, 2001 against America, in the same way that they have been motivating attacks for centuries all over the world. Now you know for sure that it was not a group of fanatics that did this thing, but real Muslims. And now you can see that the Islamic threat is real.

Readers, we ignored this teaching and the religion that teaches its followers these things for far too long. We looked the other way for years as they built for this attack right under our noses, right on our own streets of our own cities. Then one day America was blasted by The Qur'an being obeyed and we had the nerve to act shocked, surprised, and upset.

Going forward from here on out, we cannot afford to pretend that we don't know what is going on. You cannot sit here reading this and pretend that you don't know that something of the magnitude of 09-11-2001 is getting set to happen again.

My closing words of this book are addressed specifically to the Christians. We can all play a role in this great crusade, no matter where we are located and no matter how big or small our churches are.

Brothers and sisters in Christ around the world, it is time to act. Don't allow what is happening in America to happen to your nation as well. Confront the evil of Islam wherever and whenever it rears its ugly head, no matter what the secular world may say about you for it!

To Christians in the inner-city Christian churches in America, let's work together to evangelize the lost Muslims. Go out onto the streets of your town and walk over to the Islamic community (don't act like you don't know where this neighborhood is located either). If you didn't know where the Islamic community or the Muslim neighborhood in your city is, shame on you. Find it and go there with the truth.

To you pastors and lay people in the suburban American churches, let me tell you something. Whether you like it or not, whether you believe it or not, Islam is coming to your town. It may take 20 years or it may take 3 years. It may already be starting to arrive as you sit here reading this. Ignoring it will not keep it from showing up. And pretending it does not exist does not help any of the lost who are trapped in it. It is your duty to know how to witness to them! Read up and study about it now so that when they build a mosque or an Islamic center down the block from you (it could happen in a month for all you know), you are not caught off guard and stuck for an answer. While you sit back and build coffee shops and mega churches with video game arcades in them, Muslims are hitting the books and learning all of the classic Islamic arguments well. Can you dialogue with them meaningfully? If not, get on it now. Also give financially on a regular basis to the inner-city outreach ministries who are on the front line of the major city nearest to you. My suggestion is to pick one, two, three, or however many God has prospered you to support, and then commit yourselves to helping them out regularly.

To our brothers and sisters in the rural parts of America, the odds are good that Islam will not cross your path for a decade or more, if at all. You have much more time to work with in order to train your saints. Go ahead and begin the task slowly and thoroughly, so that if in a future generation Islam comes to your small town, your people will be more than equipped to deal with it and stomp it out in its infancy. And also please pray for the pastors, teachers, and congregations of the inner-city and suburban Christian churches of America. Even if you never encounter Islam in your life, you have brothers and sisters in other parts of your state who deal with it on a daily basis. Your prayers can be their ultimate secret weapon in the struggle! Your financial support to counter-cult ministries in the major cities and their surrounding communities can give them a big lift as well. The fight is everyone's, including yours. I hope to see you all step up in the coming years and make a contribution that God will be pleased with!

To my Christian brothers and sisters in prison, know that you are not forgotten about. But also know that you, your Christian brothers, and your non-Christian neighbors right there in prison with you are seen by Muslims as prey. Many of the most radical Muslims I've ever met were converted in prison. You're right there, so I know you know what I am talking about when I say that the movement in there is extremely aggressive. You are where you are at this moment for a reason. God has placed you there. Our society may have locked you up and thrown away the key, and it may seem like you are forgotten about. But rest assured that God the Creator has not forgotten about you! You have a job to do right there in that place.

The fiercest battleground between Islam and Christianity right now in our country is in the prison system. And you are our soldiers on the front lines. Write to churches and Christian ministries and ask them to get books and tracts to you on the inside. Get the chaplain's permission to have Faith Defenders or Impact Apologetics come into the system and give a seminar aimed at converting Muslims in prison. Try to get your hands specifically on the resources I will mention in Appendix C. When you absorb all of the knowledge that these resources can give you, the Muslims in prison will see you as untouchable in a debate. Your friends will not be converted because you'll have the words to say to stop them from making such a terrible decision. Also, find out who else in the prison system is a Christian. Hang out together in a group and protect one another as a family. No one should be forced to convert to the lie of Islam just for protection or because if they don't, they'll be assaulted. Those of you who can read, try to teach those who cannot how to read. The secular system may have given up on you, but God has not. There is still a mission for you in there. Accept it and carry it out, my brothers and sisters!

<u>To all Christians everywhere in America,</u> our government seems convinced not to see the real enemy. While our military chases the enemy in another part of the world, it is actually right here with us and is maneuvering for its next big strike against us. Dependent upon our own government to win their little **"War On Terror"**, we might as well forget it. It looks like we are the only ones who can do anything about it.

No, I'm not saying that our enemies are *the Muslim people*. Don't write me any letters about how I supposedly hate Muslims. I love Muslims. They are people who are trapped, and are not the problem. The real enemy is *the Satanic belief system of Islam* that has them chained up. As I said in the beginning, my target is not any specific group of people, but rather, I'm aimed at the spiritual forces that are guiding those people. When we can separate the Muslim from his wicked religion then he can truly be free!

What a person believes to be true ultimately affects how he lives and what choices he makes in his daily life. There are nearly 1.5 billion people on earth who absolutely believe that it is an act of servitude to their god to make war against those who do not believe in him. So those of us who do not believe in him should take that very seriously, and we should understand that there is real cause for concern. We should be moved towards some kind of counter-action against this before it is too late.

Christians united (only unity around the truth is real unity) are more unstoppable than all of the planes and all of the suicide bombers in the entire Middle East put together! Let's reach as many Muslims as possible with the truth before the lie comes back to haunt our country again.

CLOSING PRAYER

Dear God, please bless America and keep her standing for as long as You see fit. We, Your church, stand unified and ready as willing tools, desiring to be used by You in this battle against Islam. Please do Your will through us, and please give us the strength to make it through the struggle victoriously, as well as the wisdom to do it in a way that pleases You.

Amen.

Brian James Shanley

APPENDIX A

The Muslim Concept Of Heaven As A Motivational Factor Which Results In Acts Of Terrorism

"And those who are slain in the way of God, He will not send their works astray. He will guide them, and dispose their minds aright, and He will admit them to Paradise, that which He has made known to them."

[SURA 47:4-6]

Hello, readers! Just when you thought you made it through my book you get hit with more. Well, what you're about to read was originally going to be a separate booklet that I was going to hand out on the streets of The Twin Cities, MN for the purpose of informing everyone about what is going on.

But instead, I have decided to provide it here as an appendix for a bonus to you. You deserve to own a book that is as jam-packed with as much information as possible. Thank you for your support in having purchased this book. I really hope you have enjoyed it and have learned a lot from it as well.

LAS VEGAS HAS NOTHING ON THE MUSLIM HEAVEN

Contrary to The Bible's account of the 3rd heaven being a place of holiness (it is the specific dwelling place of God, who is an essentially holy being), The Qur'an paints a picture of heaven like a gross, wicked, and sinful city.

Even a resident of Las Vegas, NV, USA would say, *"Dang! That's one wicked place."*

THEY CANNOT WAIT TO GET THERE – SUICIDE MISSIONS HELP SPEED UP THE PROCESS

Once I begin to describe it in a moment, you will begin to understand why so many young Muslim men have absolutely no problem strapping some dynamite onto their chests, getting on a crowded bus full of men, women, and children, and then detonating it. You see, since The Qur'an commands Muslims to commit acts of jihad (holy war) against infidels (non-Muslims), when they are killed in obedience to these commands they believe they will go straight to the Muslim heaven. They're excited about it. They look forward to it. Why is that? Let us open up The Qur'an once again to see what is waiting there for them after they die while rendering this service to Allah.

WHEN A RELIGION CANNOT TELL THE DIFFERENCE BETWEEN ITS HEAVEN AND A BAR, THAT SAYS A LOT ABOUT THE RELIGION

> *"This is the similitude of Paradise which the godfearing have been promised: therein are rivers of water unstaling, rivers of milk unchanging in flavour, and rivers of wine – a delight to the drinkers,"*
>
> *[SURA 47:15]*

This is perhaps one of the only accurate things that Muhammad has ever said. Anyone who in this earthly lifetime has had some wine or some alcohol will agree with him. It sure is a delight to the drinkers! It makes you enter into the drunken state if you have too much of it.

In other parts of The Qur'an it describes the drunken state that the Muslim is supposedly going to be in once he arrives in heaven and drinks.

> *"Surely the pious shall be in bliss,"*
>
> **[SURA 83:22]**

Now we may run into problems. If you are reading this and you happen to be a liberal Muslim, you're going to interpret this "bliss" as a figure of speech, describing how happy the righteous Muslims will be in Allah's heaven. And you'll definitely come against my interpretation.

But the context of Sura 83 is clear. Heaven is being discussed in a literal way throughout the whole thing. One cannot interpret the rest of it literally and then decide that only the "bliss" portion is a figure of speech. This is inconsistent. A contextual reading of the sura points us in the right direction. It is quite clear what is going on in the passage. The righteous Muslims are there in a "blissful" or drunken state. And the cause of this blissful drunkenness is the wine. If you still disagree with me, keep on reading Sura 83.

> *"thou knowest in their faces the radiancy of bliss as they are given to drink of a wine sealed whose seal is musk – so after that let the strivers strive – and whose mixture is Tasnim, a fountain at which do drink those brought nigh."*
>
> **[SURA 83:24-28]**

Notice the reference to a heavenly alcoholic fountain, sort of "Allah's cosmic tap" from which Muslims will spend eternity drinking wine. This is how they will enter into the drunken bliss. Let's go back to Ali for some light on the alcohol in heaven.

> *"6024. The Wine will be of the utmost purity and flavour,"*
>
> **THE QUR'AN: TEXT, TRANSLATION, AND COMMENTARY**, *by Abdullah Yusuf Ali, Footnote # 6024, page 1706, Tahrike Tarsile Qur'an, Inc., 1934*
> *ISBN 094 036 8323*

He does not deny that *literal wine will be in heaven.* Let's read his take on the alcoholic fountain out of which this wine will flow.

> *"6026. Tasnim literally indicates height, fulness, opulence. Here it is; the name of a heavenly Fountain, whose drink is superior to that of the Purest Wine. It is the nectar drunk by Those Nearest to God (n. 5277 to lvi. 11), the highest in spiritual dignity; but a flavour of it will be given to all, according to their spiritual capacity."*
>
> **THE QUR'AN: TEXT, TRANSLATION, AND COMMENTARY**, *by Abdullah Yusuf Ali, Footnote # 6026, page 1706, Tahrike Tarsile Qur'an, Inc., 1934*
> *ISBN 094 036 8323*

He once again does not deny literal wine. He even indicates that it is a literal fountain by referring to physical characteristics like height, etc. to describe it. He says that a flavor of this wine will be given to everyone in heaven depending upon their spiritual capacity. I guess the greater of a servant you are to Allah on this earth, the more alcohol you will be allowed to drink in the Muslim heaven!

The context supports me and the most popular Qur'anic commentary in America does not contradict me when I come out and call the Muslim heaven exactly what it is – a big, drunken party.

ALLAH ALLOWS DRUNKENNESS IN HEAVEN? I THOUGHT THE QUR'AN FORBIDS ALCOHOL

It does. This is one of the errors of The Qur'an. It contradicts itself because of the difference of its teachings of heaven versus the view of alcohol that it teaches Muslims who are still living here on the earth. Check this out:

> *"O believers, wine and arrow-shuffling, idols and divining-arrows are an abomination, some of Satan's work; so avoid it; haply so you will prosper. Satan only desires to precipitate enmity and hatred between you in regard to wine and arrow-shuffling, and to bar you from the remembrance of God, and from prayer. Will you then desist?"*
>
> **[SURA 5:90+91]**

In these verses, wine (alcohol) is put on the same moral level as arrow-shuffling (gambling), idol worship (being involved in a religion other than Islam), and divining arrows (a kind of divination which was popular in Arabia in Muhammad's time). It is called "Satan's work". The Muslim is told to avoid it so they will prosper (succeed in life).

The passage went on to say that Satan was attempting to disrupt the unity between the Muslims through wine (alcohol), as well as to keep the Muslim from remembering God, and to make the Muslim forget to pray. The Muslim is then called to desist, or stay away from, alcohol. In Islam, alcohol is sinful. It is an abomination.

Can you see the problems these verses pose for one another? Can you see the contradictory nature of the Muslim life on earth and the Muslim heaven?

Muhammad was not the most intelligent man to ever have lived, that is for sure! I don't know if he spent too many hours in the desert sun, had heat stroke, and got dizzy before reciting The Qur'an to the scribes or something. But it is very clear that something went wrong with the authorship of this mess. A confused individual has given us a confused book.

Do you see the problem? Other than his idea of heaven being no better than *Dollar Drink Night* at the local bar in your town, we can see the issue of conflict about what heaven is like. And we see problems with the nature of Muhammad's concept of God.

Muhammad's Allah deity is going to have wine (alcohol), which he has declared sinful and an abomination in other parts of The Qur'an which we've just read, in heaven for all eternity. How can he do this? Especially since he has also said:

> *"They will question thee concerning wine, and arrow-shuffling. Say: 'In both is heinous sin, and uses for men, but the sin in them is more heinous than the usefulness'."*
>
> **[SURA 2:219]**

In this passage, Muslims are being made aware that non-Muslims will come up to them at times with questions about the Muslim position on certain life issues. The Muslim who reads this verse is being trained how to properly answer.

Wine once again is put on the same level as gambling. And we're told that in both are "heinous sin". Once again, my boy Ali helps out my side when he writes:

> *"240. Wine: Khamr: literally understood to mean the fermented juice of the grape; applied by analogy to all fermented liquor, and by further analogy to any intoxicating liquor or drug. There may possibly be some benefit in it, but the harm is greater than the benefit, especially if we look at it from a social as well as an individual point of view."*
>
> **THE QUR'AN: TEXT, TRANSLATION, AND COMMENTARY**, *by Abdullah Yusuf Ali, Footnote # 240, page 86, Tahrike Tarsile Qur'an, Inc., 1934*
> *ISBN 094 036 8323*

Ali agrees with the Qur'anic text that, though there may be some benefit to getting intoxicated, the bad outweighs the good and therefore it is sinful. Since Allah is supposedly the author of The Qur'an, then we can only conclude that in the sight of Allah, drunkenness is a sin.

Think for a second about what this means for The Qur'anic account of Allah's heaven. When we read about rivers of wine and drunken bliss in heaven in one sura, and then of it being a sin in another sura, then what does it mean about the one who wrote both suras?

ALLAH'S CONTRADICTORY ESSENCE

In his heaven we have wine, which is an abomination. It's Satan's handiwork. It's heinous and sinful in the sight of Allah. Yet its consumption will be going on unpunished right in front of him for all eternity! Tell me that makes sense to you! Tell me you can see no problem or no inconsistency! You cannot say that.

This big river of wine in Allah's heaven is going to cause what he calls sin to take place right in his presence for eternity. But this moon deity is going to look the other way. There is no mention of a punishment in The Qur'an for these people. As a matter of fact, he even seems to be approving of it in his description of heaven. But in other verses, like what I have just quoted above, he hates alcohol. Which is true? Either he hates alcohol and drunkenness or he approves. Muhammad can not quite make up his mind about which picture of Allah to paint.

Brian James Shanley

ALLAH'S IMPERFECT ESSENCE

If the account of his heaven described in The Qur'an is accurate, then Islam's god Allah is imperfect. He is what we call a finite (limited) god. In order to be perfect, Allah has to be perfect in all ways and in all attributes. But if his heaven will be one big drunken alcohol fest of partaking in what he has already called "Satan's handiwork" - and if this will happen right in his presence but he allows it to go on unpunished for all eternity, then he is less than perfect in the area of justice. Perfect justice demands punishment for every sin. The failure to punish even one sin is imperfect justice by definition.

Or if there is gross sin taking place in heaven and he merely looks past it for all eternity, and can even co-exist with it right in his own dwelling place, then he fails to be perfect in the area of holiness. A true holy God is violated when he looks upon sin. Muhammad's Allah god seems unbothered by eternal sin in his face. Allah is then an unholy god.

So, as we have just seen, Allah is limited in either justice or holiness. Whichever one you want to call him, take your pick. We still have a less than perfect picture of god in Islam being painted by the Islamic concept of heaven.

If you are a Muslim reading this, you really have to think about that. Do you really want such an imperfect god dictating the course of your life? You don't need such a deity guiding you. You cannot lean on, trust, or depend upon a god who is imperfect like Allah is.

I highly encourage you to renounce him, his counterfeit book, and his false prophet today and come to the knowledge and acceptance of the truth of Christianity. The One True God who always has existed and always will exist eternally as Father, Son, and Holy Spirit desires a relationship with you. He is not a God who will fail you. Allah obviously has problems.

ALLAH'S HEAVENLY HOES

Not only does the Muslim terrorist have rivers of liquor and a drunken bliss to look forward to, but he has eternal sex awaiting him as well.

"Surely the godfearing shall be in gardens and bliss, rejoicing in that their Lord has given them; and their Lord shall guard them against the chastisement of Hell. 'Eat and drink, with wholesome appetite, for that you were working'. Reclining upon couches ranged in rows; and We shall espouse them to wide-eyed houris."

[SURA 52:17-20]

"Surely the godfearing" – What god is in view? Allah. Those who fear (respect, obey, and worship) him are in view. Muslims. *"shall be in gardens"* – If they die having obeyed the pillars of Islam, and if Allah feels like letting them in, they'll be in heaven. *"and bliss,"* – Drunk as a skunk. *"rejoicing in that their Lord has given them;"* – They're happy to be there. *"and their Lord shall guard them against the chastisement of Hell."* – Hell is the opposite of heaven. Another good indicator that heaven is in view in this passage. The righteous Muslim will be kept from hell. *"'Eat and drink, with wholesome appetite'* - Notice all of the allusions to human physical appetites.

Allah's heaven is kind of a carnal place, isn't it? It appeals to the flesh in a big way, doesn't it? ***"for that you were working'"*** – The real motive behind all terrorism, all persecution of non-Muslim people or religions, or anything that Muslims do is finally revealed. It is simply to get there and receive these things. ***"Reclining upon couches ranged in rows;"*** – And so far nothing has been presented in the text to lead us to believe that this is not to be taken as a literal couch. Everything thus far has been a *physical* description of a *literal* place, even to the point of referring to human appetites of the physical body. Could a couch really be a figure of speech or an analogy about anything anyway? What would it symbolize? Ha, ha, ha! ***"and We"*** – Allah is referring to himself in the plural. This is usually done to represent majesty or royalty. ***"shall espouse them to wide-eyed houris."*** – The question is: What's a houri? Well, another way we sometimes write it is *hori*. When we put it into English, we say *whore*. Some of our brothers in the inner-cities leave out the letter "R" and just say *hoe*. It is used of a woman that people do not value very much at all. It is associated with a person whose only purpose or desire in life is to sexually please men. They have no other purpose and no other plans. This kind of woman is seen as good for nothing else in the world. It is a derogatory term today and considered an insult for a woman to be called either a whore or a hoe.

So in Allah's heaven Muslims not only do you get to drink from a river of alcohol and get to remain absolutely wasted for all eternity, but you also get to have eternal sex by being joined to Allah's heavenly hoes. Allah even goes on to say:

> *"And We shall succour them with fruits and flesh such as they desire."*
>
> **[SURA 52:22]**

More references to both food and flesh. Being given as much *flesh* as they want really means as much *sex* as they want. It is carnality run wild!

Islam is merely the abstaining from wickedness for a lifetime in exchange for an eternity of immeasurably more wickedness than they could have gotten access to during their entire stay on the earth! It is sin delayed, but not denied!

This is a brilliant religion that Satan has designed. It certainly does its job well, and appeals to people's sin nature from within in order to get them following after a false god and a false religious system, by dangling a carrot of a wicked heaven in front of their faces. So far today in 2002 nearly a billion and a half have been suckered in through teachings like this.

Let's look at more help from Abdullah Yusuf Ali.

> *"5058....There is no question of sex in heaven."*
>
> **THE QUR'AN: TEXT, TRANSLATION, AND COMMENTARY**, *by Abdullah Yusuf Ali, Footnote # 5058, page 1436, Tahrike Tarsile Qur'an, Inc., 1934 ISBN 094 036 8323*

Could it be any plainer what is being taught about?

Brian James Shanley

DO YOU SEE HOW ISLAM'S CONCEPT OF HEAVEN COULD MOTIVATE TERRORISM?

Imagine if you knew that when you died that you'd have a big drunken sex party to look forward to. There is no fear of death anymore. Nothing in this world phases you because you're about to enter into something much better. There is no fear of consequences. There is no concern about the damage that you're about to do to the people who you will leave behind. Who cares? They're back there on that planet and you're on your way to heaven. Who cares who've just hurt back there? It's all behind you now. You've got a party to get to! You've got girls waiting to have sex with you for all eternity on heavenly couches! But you'll only have a "go" at them after getting liquored up in rivers of wine!

Of course, doing something for Allah on your way out might be a grand finale! If you perform a suicide mission, it will only speed up the process and eliminate the waiting period before you enter this place. It might even earn you a great bonus when you are judged. So why not strap a bomb to yourself and take a few infidels with you on your way out of this life? Or why not make your exit be something like hijacking a plane and crashing it into a building occupied by Allah's enemies (non-Muslims)?

This kind of a heaven provides that kind of mental attitude to Muslims and potential terrorists. When you combine the mental attitude produced by this heaven with all of the jihads declared in Muslim countries against America, it is clear to see that Islam will be able to produce

140

more anti-American soldiers to participate in more terrorist attacks against us for generations to come.

As I've said before, September 11th, 2001 was just the beginning.

LIKE THE ALCOHOLIC FESTIVAL PORTION OF HEAVEN, THE SEX PARTY PORTION OF HEAVEN ALSO RUNS INTO PROBLEMS UPON EXAMINATION

The first problem with it is the "ceremonial impurity" which, according to The Qur'an, comes from the act of sex. The Qur'an talks about an elaborate cleaning process that the Muslim here on the earth has to go through after sex. (S)he has to do this just to be able to qualify to approach Allah! It's really ridiculous, but it is in The Qur'an and we're getting set to read about it.

Before prayer, they have to enter into what is known as *wudhu*. It's a state one must enter into before Islam's god will even bother to listen to you. It's all about total physical cleanliness. I've never fully understood why they believe it. Prayer is a *spiritual* thing, yet for some reason they have to *physically* clean themselves to pray. I guess you can be as *spiritually dirty* as you want, but as long as you are *physically clean* you are all good! Kind of a backwards focus, but this is how Islam teaches.

141

Check out The Qur'an:

> *"O believers, when you stand up to pray wash your faces, and your hands up to the elbows, and wipe your heads, and your feet up to the ankles. If you are defiled, purify yourselves;"*
>
> *[SURA 5:6]*

Basically this verse is teaching the Muslim how to enter into this "wudhu" state so that Al-Ilah will listen to them. Imagine a god who loves his people so little that listening to their prayers is conditional, and based upon their physical cleanliness! Amazing.

Anyways, that term saying "***if you are defiled, purify yourselves***" is translated by Abdullah Yusuf Ali like this: "***If ye are in a state of ceremonial impurity, bathe your whole body***". The idea is that the physical act of sex leaves one physically dirty. This physical dirtiness disconnects one from being able to get a prayer through to their god Allah. So before attempting to pray to him, they need to get rid of this physical dirtiness. Check out Ali's footnote for more light as to how a Muslim scholar sees this issue:

> *"703. Cf. iv. 43 and n. 563. Ceremonial impurity arises from sex pollution."*
>
> **THE QUR'AN: TEXT, TRANSLATION, AND COMMENTARY**,
> *By Abdullah Yusuf Ali, Footnote # 703, page 242, Tahrike Tarsile Qur'an, Inc., 1934*
> *ISBN 094 036 8323*

Ali calls the physical condition one is in following sex "sex pollution"! This renders the Muslim too dirty to approach Allah in prayer, and therefore the cleaning process described in The Qur'an is necessary. If you've had sex recently and you're a Muslim, you have to bathe your whole body before you can even talk to Allah! Is that wild or what?

Knowing this about the teachings Islam puts forth concerning sex, it raises an interesting question about the Islamic concept of heaven. If physical sex down here on the earth blocks the Muslim from being clean enough to approach Allah in prayer, then why is it one of the main activities right in his dwelling place in heaven?

If you're on a couch having eternal sex with one of the heavenly hoes we've discussed earlier right in Allah's face, how can he look favorably upon you? You're "sex polluting" yourself right before him!

If sex makes you too dirty to talk to him *from far away*, then certainly it makes you too dirty to be *in his presence* for all eternity!

A HOMOSEXUAL'S PARADISE?

In 1995 rap singer Coolio put out a song called *"Gangster's Paradise"*. The song described his life and times growing up as a kid in a certain inner-city neighborhood. In this particular neighborhood, there were drugs and gangs. These kinds of surroundings led him to refer to that place as a *"Gangster's Paradise"*.

Well, the surroundings in the Muslim heaven have similarly led me to refer to Allah's dwelling place as *"Homosexual's Paradise"*. This is because that, as I've researched this issue, I've discovered another bizarre part of the Qur'anic teaching concerning heaven.

Not only will there be *women to commit fornication with* for eternity, but there also will be *young men to commit sodomy with*. This is absolutely sick. Check out The Qur'an. I've already quoted this passage in part to demonstrate the sexual nature of the Muslim concept of eternity. Now I will quote the passage in full to demonstrate that a portion of the sexual nature of the Muslim concept of heaven is actually homosexual!

> *"We shall succour them with fruits and flesh such as they desire while they pass therein a cup to one another wherein is no idle talk, no cause of sin, and there go round them youths, their own, as it they were hidden pearls."*
>
> **[SURA 52:22-24]**

In case this does not give you the full flavor, let us also get Abdullah Yusuf Ali's translation of verses 23 & 24 of this passage.

> *"They shall there exchange, one with another a (loving) cup free of frivolity, free of all taint of ill. Round about them will serve, (devoted) to them, youths (handsome) as Pearls well-guarded."*
>
> **[SURA 52:23 + 24, Ali's Translation]**

The fact that there are youths in heaven devoted to the Muslim male for service can be easily seen when one looks back at verse 22 and sees the context. It reveals the capacity in which these youths will serve.

Providing the Muslim ***"flesh such as they desire"*** is clearly the focus of what is going on here, and verses 23 + 24 are an expansion on that idea. The analogy of the youths being described as well-guarded pearls is a reference to virginity. Since in the ***"Allah's Heavenly Hoes"*** section of this book we saw that *the women* available to male Muslims are virgins, it is consistent and fitting that *the young men* available to male Muslims are virgins as well.

No man has ever sodomized these youths before, and the Muslim man entering heaven is going to he the 1st one to have that opportunity. So, in a sick sense, the youths' "virginity" will have been preserved just for the Muslim male until he gets to heaven. Virginity is a valuable thing because, once lost, it cannot be gotten back. It is therefore a thing to be desired. So a valuable thing like a pearl is a good description of it. And the fact that this pearl has been well-guarded indicates that it has been protected and preserved.

And describing the men as "young" indicates that they'll be in excellent shape and physically appealing to any Muslim male that is attracted to other males.

In many Islamic countries, the rape of young boys by older men is all too common. Some of them get sodomized so badly, so often, and over so long of a period of time that they eventually lose their sexual orientation. They become numb to this sort of thing, even to the point of thinking that it is an acceptable practice. Sex becomes a random act that can be had with anyone, male or female. And when they grow up, they pass it on to the next generation of young boys. This is a documented fact in many Islamic writings.

In his description of heaven, Muhammad was trying to appeal to so broad of an audience that he even included something waiting there for the many men who desired young boys. To this day, the Muslim suicide bomber not only looks forward to rivers of liquor and heavenly prostitute women, but also the sodomizing of young males for eternal homosexual gratification.

> *"There is no question of sex in heaven. But the type of the grace and gentleness of womanhood having been applied in the word Hur (verse 20 above), the type of the handsome and well-formed strength and splendor of manhood is mentioned here in the allegory of Pearls, - of the purest water, well-guarded from weathering and unsullied by rough usage."*
>
> **THE QUR'AN - TEXT, TRANSLATION, AND COMMENTARY**, *by Abdullah Yusuf Ali, Footnote 5058, page 1436, Tahrike Tarsile Qur'an, Inc., 1934*
> *ISBN 094 036 8323*

Of the verse about the youths, Ali even says that ***"there is no question of sex in heaven"***. The same way that the prior verses I've cited refer to the Muslim males' use of the "houris" is the same way that the youths are spoken of here.

They are the most handsome and in the best possible physical shape, and their virginity has been protected and preserved, having been guarded against ***"rough usage"***. I guess the newly-deceased Muslim male will be the 1st one ever to get to apply the ***"rough usage"*** to the youth.

This is vile and disgusting. But to the Islamic terrorist who is into that sort of thing, he is motivated to kill and be killed and go to the Muslim heaven so he can have the 1st shot at young, untouched boys. Sick! Sick! Sick!

THE FINAL VERDICT ABOUT THE ISLAMIC HEAVEN

We've seen how the human lusts and physical appetites that reside within every human heart are the focus of Islam's heaven.

It's like an exchange. Basically, Allah's heaven says to the Muslim: *"You deny these things during your earthly life, and then I'll let you have them during your eternal life."*

Since you are not chasing these things during your stay on the earth, instead you are fighting in Allah's great cause of spreading Islam. If you die while doing it, then you get to go to this heaven. As a matter of fact, since getting into heaven through any other method is conditional based solely upon *"If Allah wills it"* and there is no assurance of salvation, participating in this kind of warfare is seemingly the best way to go. It is a guarantee of a place in heaven.

147

If a person waits to die a natural death before getting to enjoy this evil paradise, they may have to hang on for nearly a century! That's nearly a century of pretending to be moral and pious and law-abiding, while inwardly burning with unsatisfied lusts for things like alcohol and fornication. That's an entire lifetime of working a job in the secular workplace, raising a family, and suffering through what people go through during the course of a normal human life.

But if they blow themselves up and take some non-Muslims with them, it'll come quicker and the reward will be better because of their obedience to the Qur'anic jihad passages.

This kind of heaven and this seemingly easy way out of the present task of life is the top reason why Islam will have no problem recruiting as many terrorists as are necessary, for as many decades as it takes, to topple the West.

The only way to stop it is to offer an alternative system of belief other than Islam. The alternative of the truth. The truth of Biblical Christianity and the real heaven, not the heaven of Muhammad's sick and sinful imagination!

Brian James Shanley

APPENDIX
B

Roots: Why They Hate Us So Much

Scripture taken from the NEW AMERICAN STANDARD BIBLE, Copyright 1960, 1962, 1963, 1968, 1971, 1972, 1973, 1975, 1977, 1994 by The Lockman Foundation. Used by permission.

PEOPLE ASK ME ALL THE TIME

I study the area of Islam in order to learn how to reach Muslims with the truth. People who know me see this, and have always asked me the question: *"Brian, I just want to know one thing. Why do they hate us so much? What did we ever do to them?"* They're referring, of course, to the Muslim nations who are always plotting ways to attempt to make our country crumble.

And this is a very valid question. The United States of America, with all of its problems, is still the most generous nation in the history of the world. We give more money out in foreign aide than some nations make during the course of a year! We send out our military to promote peace around the world, and to keep the thugs, gangsters, and dictators from oppressing the little guys all the time. Who'd want to hurt us and why?

THE QUESTION ACTUALLY HAS AN ANSWER, BUT NOT A SIMPLE ONE

When I respond to this question, I cannot just do it in passing. I usually have to end up buying the person lunch (so quit asking, because I'm getting poorer all the time! Just kidding! Ha, ha, ha!) because the answer, though understandable, cannot be easily or quickly explained. Addressing that question could become *its own book* all by itself.

I will attempt to do it in this appendix as briefly and as simply as I am able to do. It will shed light on the whole Middle Eastern problem for you as well.

IT IS NOT POLITICAL - IT IS RELIGIOUS

We can send as many of our representatives and our politicians out to the Middle East as we want. We can have "peace talks" until we are blue in the face. We can slap small, primitive Middle Eastern countries around with our military might until we own some of the land in that part of the world. It is all futile and for absolutely nothing. You cannot solve a problem when you do not have a correct understanding of the problem. This is where our country is going wrong.

The problem is not political. So a political solution will never work.

The problem is not military. Therefore for a military solution will never work.

If someone shot you in the stomach with a gun, would you put a band-aid on it? Or would you rush to a hospital and have an operation to remove the bullet, which is the root of the problem?

When we use our "peace talks" and our military to handle business in the Middle East, we treat a gunshot wound by putting a band-aid on it. We never address the actual problem. We just try to soften the effects and symptoms of that actual problem.

The reason why America is hated throughout the Middle East is not political. It is not military. It is spiritual. It is religious. Specifically, the religion of Islam.

Remember what I wrote earlier on? What a person believes to be the truth ultimately affects the way that they live and the decisions that they make. Islam teaches them to hate us and our way of life.

In the following paragraphs, if you read them chronologically (in order) from start to finish, you'll have your answer. Keep in mind that the problem is religious in nature and therefore at times Biblical texts are quoted to help illustrate.

1. ABRAHAM (THEN CALLED ABRAM) WAS PROMISED BY GOD THAT HE'D HAVE A SON

"After these things the word of the LORD came to Abram in a vision, saying, 'Do not fear, Abram, I am a shield to you; Your reward shall be very great'. Abram said, 'O Lord God, what will you give me, since I am childless, and the heir of my house is Eliezer of Damascus?' And Abram said, 'Since You have given no offspring to me, one born in my house is my heir'. Then behold, the word of the LORD came to him, saying, 'This man will not be your heir; but one who shall come forth from your own body, he shall be your heir'. And He took him outside and said, 'Now look toward the heavens, and count the stars, if you are able to count them'. And He said to him, 'So shall your descendants be'."

[GENESIS 15:1-5]

After dealing with the lie of The Qur'an for nearly this whole book, what a breath of fresh air to have a quote from the truth of The Bible in here!

In this Biblical verse God told Abram that his reward was going to be great. Abram had trouble getting excited about it, because he did not have any children to leave any rewards to as an inheritance after he died. He referred to Eliezer of Damascus as his heir because if he couldn't leave anything to a blood-related child, he'd have to use one of his servants as the heir to receive his estate.

But God promised him that not only would He reward him, but He would give Abram more descendants than could be counted!

2. *ABRAHAM (STILL CALLED ABRAM) WAS PROMISED A PIECE OF LAND TO LEAVE BEHIND TO HIS SON AND TO ALL OF HIS SON'S DESCENDANTS*

"And He said to him, 'I am the LORD who brought you out of Ur of the Chaldeans, to give you this land to possess it."

[GENESIS 15:7}

"On that day the LORD made a covenant with Abram, saying, 'To your descendants I have given this land, from the river of Egypt as far as the great river, the river Euphrates: the Kenite and the Kenizzite and the Kadmonite and the Hittite and the Perizzite and the Girgashite and the Jebusite'."

[GENESIS 15:18-21]

The descendants of Abram, who we today know as "the Jews", have been promised this piece of land. It has not been promised to anyone else.

3. ABRAHAM (CALLED ABRAM AT THIS POINT) WAS GETTING OLDER AND STILL NO HEIR HAD BEEN BORN AS GOD HAD PROMISED - SO HE GOT IMPATIENT AND TOOK MATTERS INTO HIS OWN HANDS

We've all been there (those of us who believe in God). We're waiting on God to bless us with a certain thing, like a spouse or a material possession or something, and we (being human beings) eventually get tired of waiting. We go out and attempt to get our wants by ourselves, apart from God, by our own means. And what happens? It usually explodes in our face. We should've waited on God to bring it to us in His own time!

Even Abraham went through this. He was getting older and older. Still no child was born. He couldn't have any descendants without a son, could he? So he and his wife Sarah (then called Sarai) decided that Abram should try to conceive by their Egyptian maid, Hagar.

> *"Now Sarai, Abram's wife had borne him no children, and she had an Egyptian maid whose name was Hagar. So Sarai said to Abram, 'Now behold, the LORD has prevented me from bearing children. Please go into my maid; perhaps I shall obtain children through her'. And Abram listened to the voice of Sarai. After Abram had lived ten years in the land of Canaan, Abram's wife Sarai took Hagar the Egyptian, her maid, and gave her to her husband Abram as his wife. He went into Hagar, and she conceived;"*
> *[GENESIS 16:1-4a]*

This caused a problem between Sarai and Hagar. Sarai was upset because this other woman had conceived for her husband but she had been unable to. She began to mistreat Hagar so badly that Hagar felt the need to run away. One can imagine the many emotions she must've felt, being pregnant with the child of another woman's husband, and then having to answer to that woman on a daily basis! As the discouragement Hagar was feeling reached a peak level, God showed up! Even back in those days, God was always right on time!

> *"Now the angel of the LORD found her by a spring of water in the wilderness, by the spring on the way to Shur. He said, 'Hagar, Sarai's maid, where have you come from and where are you going?' And she said, 'I am fleeing from the presence of my mistress Sarai'. The the angel of the LORD said to her, 'Return to your mistress, and submit yourself to her authority'. Moreover, the angel of the LORD said to her, 'I will greatly multiply your descendants so that they shall be too many to count'. The angel of the LORD said to her further, 'Behold, you are with child; And you shall bear a son; And you shall call his name Ishmael, because the LORD has given heed to your affliction. He will be a wild donkey of a man, his hand will be against everyone, and everyone's hand will be against him; And he will live to the east of all his brothers'."*
>
> **[GENESIS 16:7-12]**

Hagar was instructed by the Messenger of YHWH (Who is a book subject all by Himself as well) to return back to where she ran away from and be in subjection to Sarai again. She was to raise this baby and call him Ishmael.

155

Ishmael was also going to have descendants. Was he the heir that Abraham was looking to have?

4. ISHMAEL WAS NOT THE SON THAT GOD HAD PROMISED TO ABRAHAM

As Abram was getting circumcised (and his name was changed to Abraham at this point), God once again promised his descendants this piece of land.

> *"I will give to you and to your descendants after you, the land of your sojournings, all the land of Canaan, for an everlasting possession; and I will be their God."*
>
> ### [GENESIS 17:8]

This time Abraham could be happy about this offer, because he now had the son necessary in order to have descendants. Surely this child Ishmael would be the heir to the promise, and surely his descendants would have the God-given right to occupy this land. He even approached God about Ishmael being the child through whom this promise would be fulfilled.

> *"And Abraham said to God, 'Oh that Ishmael might live before you'!"*
>
> ### [GENESIS 17:18]

It makes sense in a way, doesn't it? If a man's descendants are promised a certain piece of land and he only has one son at that time, then most of us can see Abraham's side. That one son seemed like the one through whom the descendants would come and occupy this "promised land".

You will be surprised by God's response in the very next verse.

> *"But God said, 'No, but **Sarah your wife** shall bear you a son, and you shall call his name **Isaac**; and I will establish My covenant with **him** for an everlasting covenant for **his** descendants after **him**."*
>
> ### *[GENESIS 17:19]*

Any bold-faced type or underlining in the text above is not in The Bible, but was added by me for the purpose of emphasis. In contrast to Abraham's statement about Ishmael, God plainly says "No" and even corrects Abraham's statement.

The child of the promise would not come from Hagar the Egyptian slave, but from his wife Sarah (she was no longer called Sarai anymore by now) instead. And this kid would not be called Ishmael, but Isaac. And all of the promises that God had made to Abraham and Abraham's descendants would be fulfilled through Isaac and his children, not Ishmael and his children.

> *"But **My covenant I will establish with Isaac**, whom Sarah will bear to you at this season next year."*
>
> ### *[GENESIS 17:21]*

Once again, any bold-faced type or underlining in the above verse is not in The Bible, but was added by me for the purpose of emphasis.

Look at the emphasized text. Could it be written any plainer in the Scriptures?

5. ISAAC WAS THE SON THAT GOD HAD PROMISED ABRAHAM

By the time Isaac was born, Ishmael was a little bit older. We don't know his exact age, but we knew he was old enough to comprehend what was going on around him. As Ishmael saw this new baby born to Abraham through his actual wife, he must've been crushed. His inheritance was not actually his after all, but belonged to his little half-brother instead.

In Genesis 21:9 we see that Ishmael gets jealous of little Isaac and begins to mock him. In the next verse Sarah, in defense of her baby, confronts her husband Abraham about the issue.

> *"Therefore she said to Abraham, 'Drive out this maid and her son, for the son of this maid shall not be an heir with my son Isaac'."*
>
> *[GENESIS 21:10]*

She was right. Ishmael was not the heir. He was the product of people who did not act out of faith. They did not wait on God to bless them with a child like He said He would, but instead went out by their own means to conceive a child their own way, according to their own time table. Ishmael was merely a consequence of that.

This tore Abraham up inside because he loved Ishmael. Ishmael was his kid. He didn't know what to do about it. Who does a person choose in that position? Their spouse or their child? At just the right moment, God provided Abraham some words. These words reveal even deeper that it is Isaac, not Ishmael, whose descendants would one day have that piece of land as their own.

> *"But God said to Abraham, 'Do not be distressed because of the lad and your maid; whatever Sarah tells you, listen to her, for **through Isaac your descendants shall be named**'."*
>
> *[GENESIS 21:12]*

Sorry to repeat the same stuff over and over again, but I have to say it to you. Anything in the verse above that has been highlighted through underlining or bold-facing is of me, and not in The Bible. I've done it for the purpose of emphasis.

Notice the emphasized text. It was okay to let Hagar and Ishmael go away, because his real heir was Isaac and not Ishmael.

God did promise Abraham in the next verse (Genesis 21:13) that Ishmael would be the father of a nation as well, just for being Abraham's son. But the covenant and the promise of that certain piece of land was to Abraham's descendants specifically through Isaac.

6. THE NEW TESTAMENT ALSO ADDRESSES THIS ISSUE

In the book of Galatians, Paul eventually refers to the Abraham/Sarah/Hagar/Ishmael/Isaac incident that we've just examined.

He uses it as a figurative example of how the Christian concept of justification by grace, through faith in Christ alone is superior to the Jewish Law that the Judiazers were trying to put the people back under.

> *"Tell me, you who want to be under the law, do you not listen to the law? For it is written that Abraham had two sons, one by the bondwoman and one by the free woman. But the son by the bondwoman was born according to the flesh, and the son by the free woman through the promise."*
>
> ### *[GALATIANS 4:21-23]*

Paul goes on to finish out chapter 4 of Galatians by making an application to the Christian life today. Without offering a commentary on The Book of Galatians, let me just say that The Bible speaks with a unified voice that the heir of the promise is Isaac and not Ishmael.

Ishmael was *born according to the flesh*, or according to acts of the sin nature.

Isaac was *born through the promise*, or because God promised Abraham an heir to inherit this piece of land.

7. EVENTUALLY MUHAMMAD CAME ONTO THE SCENE AND TAUGHT THE ARABS THAT THEY WERE ABRAHAM'S DESCENDANTS AND HIS RIGHTFUL HEIRS

In the 7th century, a man named Muhammad rose to power in Arabia. He was born into a major city called Mecca. Since this town was on a trade route, people passed through all the time. As different people came through town from different places, they all had different stories to tell him.

He learned a little bit about what the Jews believe, what the Christians believe, and various other religions. He could not read, so he never had the opportunity to look at a Bible or a Torah (which explains a lot of the problems in his Qur'an).

Having grown up in a polytheistic setting, the idea of monotheism sounded like a new thing. One day he took the deity of his tribe called Al-Ilah (the god of the moon) and began to preach him as the only god. He began to claim to be a prophet (mouthpiece) of this god.

Early on in his ministry he did not have the amount of followers needed to make up an army, so there was a brief period of several years where he was actually nice to people who did not accept what he said.

161

When the Jews and the Christians came through his town, they did not accept his claims of prophethood because he was not descended from Abraham through Isaac.

He could not get away with passing himself off as a Jew, so he went another direction. He said that he was descended from the line of Abraham, but through the line of Ishmael! And since he was descended from Abraham, he was a prophet of the God of Abraham. He began to claim that his Al-Ilah moon deity and the God of Abraham were one and the same. Muslims still think that to this day. Even today, Muslims and even some liberal Christians and Jews think that Islam is closely related to Christianity and Judaism. They call these three religions "the Abrahamic faiths"! Is that a riot, or what?

Taking the position of a prophet, he taught anyone who would listen that all Arabs were descendants of Abraham through the line of Ishmael. People who study the Middle East will tell you that this teaching was original with Muhammad and that, prior to Muhammad, there is no writing in ancient Arabia which calls Ishmael the father of the Arabs. This was something Muhammad just needed to invent at the spur of the moment in order to sell Islam to Jews and Christians.

He added a twist to it. Contrary to The Bible, which teaches that Isaac's descendants deserve the land of Israel, Muhammad began to teach that his Arabs, now calling themselves descendants of Ishmael, were the rightful heirs of this land.

The legend took off from there and to this day, the Arabs say that they are descended from Abraham through the line of Ishmael and that makes Israel their inheritance.

8. TO THIS DAY, THE MUSLIMS THINK THAT THIS LAND IS THEIR INHERITANCE FROM GOD AND WANT TO OCCUPY IT ALONE

Islam spread like cancer all over the Middle East and even into Africa once Muhammad got enough people to create an army. Muslims (particularly from Arab nations) believe that in the end, they will possess the land of Israel, with Jerusalem as their capital city. They're trying to bring it about however they can. They're totally self-deceived, but they think that this land is their God-given inheritance. Since it is the cause of who they feel is God, they are emotionally charged up and will stop at nothing.

The Jews to this day have not given up the Scriptural truth that this land is theirs. So between these two groups there will be nothing but war for all time until Jesus Christ returns to set it straight. He will give it to the descendants of Abraham through Isaac (the Jews), like it is supposed to be.

9. *AMERICA KEEPS ON GETTING INVOLVED*

I am all for the cause of freedom and peace all around the world. And I'm glad that America uses her power for good and not for evil. I'm glad that we recognize that the city of Jerusalem is a "hot spot" and attempt to help Israel out.

But when we get involved on the levels that we get involved on, there are going to be consequences.

Since the argument between the two sides is over the same piece of land that Abraham was promised thousands of years ago by God, there is not going to be any kind of compromise ever achieved! Both sides feel entitled to the whole place and will not budge.

When we (America) come along trying to make a compromise happen, ultimately one side or the other (or even both) will hate us for it.

10. *AMERICA KEEPS MISSING THE POINT*

I have said it about a million times in this book already. So one more time will not hurt. The problem we are up against is not political. It is not social. It is not military. It is not financial.

It is religious. It is spiritual. The minute a person abandons that, they've abandoned reality. And when one attempts to make sense out of the whole situation apart from the reality of the fact that the problem is religious in nature, they are not in a position to make any valuable contribution whatsoever to what is going on.

Not only has America abandoned the reality of the roots of what is going on over there, but we probably have never even understood in the past at any point.

We send our military over there. How can the military solve a problem that is spiritual?

We send our politicians over there to attempt to talk things out. How can politicians solve a problem that is spiritual?

You cannot solve a problem when you do not understand what it is really about. This problem has been going on over there for a long time. No political personality is going to suddenly come along and purpose something that the two sides have never seen or considered before. No one is going to convince one side or the other to go away, or to take less than the whole chunk of land.

11. IN MUSLIM COUNTRIES, THE COMMON PEOPLE ARE TAUGHT THAT AMERICANS ARE TERRORISTS

Since we get involved in the Middle East peace process a lot and never bring any real solutions to the table, the world over there is upset. The Muslim side of the argument feels like if America would butt out, then they would be freed up from the only world power bigger than they are. Therefore they would be free to get the Holy Land for Islam that they feel is their right.

They feel that the only way America will ever butt out is if America crumbled. So many of the big names in the Islamic world over in that part of the earth are trying to unite every Islamic country into one gigantic federation and come together. Yeah, they have problems with each other. So it may take a while. But it's not hard to unite themselves around one common thing: They all hate us. The minute they figure that out and come together, the rest of the world had better watch out.

The leaders of these nations come on TV and fill the common people's heads with things. In an Islamic country, there is no freedom of the press. The government controls what is on TV and in newspapers. So the TV and other media outlets in those nations paint a picture of America like it is a terrorist country that needs to be taken down.

Since the Holy Land is supposedly their birth right, the hook they use to suck people in is that they tell the masses that America is on the Jewish side of the argument! They tell them this, and we are seen as enemies who are fighting against the will of their god for their national destiny. And naturally, their response is one of anger and hatred towards America. Since Western influences in those countries are illegal, the people live in a plastic bubble. Everything they know about the world is limited to whatever sources that the Islamic government allows them access to. They're having their thoughts given to them instead of coming up with their own views of the world based upon facts.

So they're trained from early on that America is an obstacle. *"America is an enemy of Islam"* is what they are trained to learn. And they honestly believe it too!

They feel that once this "Great Satan of The West" gets taken down, the doors to The Holy Land will open up and allow them to occupy it.

It sounds sick, but it is true. If you're an American, while you read this somewhere someone is training a young kid to hate you! When this kid hits his teenage years, he'll be a cold-blooded killer. He would kill you and your family in cold blood and not even blink an eye! Elderly people and babies included. Is that scary? Imagine hundreds of thousands of people like that invading your town!

Some would suggest that the invasion started long ago, and that you pass by some of these soldiers every day on the streets, posing as regular citizens.

12. SO THEY ARE MOTIVATED AND READY TO CHALLENGE US

I hate to say it, but our society has become weak in many areas. Other countries see this and salivate. We are the dream victim because we choose not to see our attackers for who they really are, but would rather chase people around the desert in some far-away nation who had little (if anything) to do with the attack against our country. While America is not going to be defeated by this garbage, I am also saddened to say that America acts as though planes hitting the Pentagon and hitting the World Trade Center taught us nothing!

We are "sitting ducks", and perfectly open for something to happen again. It took less than a year after September 11th, 2001 for everything to die down, and for life to go right back to the way it used to be here in America prior to the attacks. We're slowly but surely going back to sleep nationally.

The Muslims see this and are just waiting for the call to come in from their handlers giving them the "green light" to go ahead - from inside of our country once again, of course.

They've got everything to gain and nothing to lose. Between the cause of advancing Islam, between the Islamic concept of heaven awaiting them, between the idea that The Holy Land should be given to the counterfeit descendants of Ishmael, and between the pure hatred for non-Muslims (American non-Muslims in particular), they have the motivation. There is great cause for concern.

September 11th, 2001 was just a warm-up to see if they could really pull it off. The next thing they hit us with is probably going to make 09-11-2001 look like Disney Land.

THE FINAL SUMMARY OF WHY THEY HATE US

Whew! What a long appendix! I told you that this was not a question with an easy answer. Here is the short version of why they hate us.

They feel like The Holy Land belongs to them and their descendants.

They are fighting the Jews over that land, to whom it rightfully belongs (we saw what The Bible says).

Because America helps the country of Israel out, the Muslims think America is on the Jews' side of the argument.

For that reason, they see us not just as an enemy of them personally, but as an enemy of their religion as well.

Their religion teaches them to kill all enemies of their religion.

Therefore they have to kill us individually, and topple us nationally. It is a way for them to serve their god.

They also feel that if America crumbled, it would be out of the Middle East peace process and then they could conquer The Holy Land without interference. America would stop helping out Israel and no one else would help them. Then the modern-day Arabs, who feel that they have descended from Abraham through Ishmael, would set up a great nation with Jerusalem as its capital city.

That is pretty much it. May God in the person of Jesus Christ make His return swiftly and deal with this. And may He preserve America through this time and open up the eyes of her citizens. May America turn her attention to The God of The Bible for direction while she still stands as a nation.

Brian James Shanley

APPENDIX C

Resources:

Equipping Christians To Take Action

CREDIT WHERE CREDIT IS DUE

As I mentioned earlier on in the book in my section in which I separated my work from the 90-day wonder books, much of what I know about Islam comes from reading the work of other people. It's true that I studied apart from these people, and have even read writings by Muslims.

But I did not even know how to properly respond to Islam until I picked up certain books. I saw my Muslim friends as these unbeatable debaters who could not be reached. I saw the Muslim arguments as too solid to crack. I was a confused mess.

But then I came across the path of some things that helped me out. And today, the opposite is true of my life that was true 7 years ago. Now it is my Muslim friends that see me as unbeatable. Now I'm able to hang in a conversation with a Muslim.

And even though I'm coming onto the scene today, Islam has been being answered by Christians since before I was ever even born! I want to pay proper respect to the works that are out there, so I'm going to give you a list of suggested resources by others who have come before me.

THE MARKET IS FLOODED - WHO SHOULD I READ ABOUT ISLAM?

It's true. After September 11th, 2001 happened, everyone on the planet that you've never heard of decided that they were an Islamic expert. They've all written books to try to cash in on the newest fad. Trying to make a buck off of your fears about terrorism. Everyone who never cared about Islam or saw the Islamic threat before 09-11-2001 had something to say afterwards. But not all of them are like that.

Having studied this for years prior to September 11th, 2001, I can say that there are good people out there to read. There are people that were concerned about Islam before it was a cultural trend. And when the trend-followers have moved on to the next thing, these warriors will still be right here, fighting to save Muslims.

If you want to read more about Islam, check out these people. They are not afraid to tell it like it is. They will not hold back on telling you the truth. They will give you a great introduction into the problems of Islam.

MY SUGGESTION TO YOU - GET AS MUCH AS YOU CAN

Are you interested in reaching Muslims? Have you read the truths in the earlier part of this book and been motivated to want to cause a change for the better? Want to take on Islam in the name of Christ to preserve America?

If so, then I want to make you a suggestion. Pick up a copy of each and every thing that I list. Depending upon how God has prospered you, you may be able to do this soon. Or, you may have to collect these things one at a time over several years. Either way is fine.

Here is my promise to you. If you go out and do this, there will not be a Muslim that you run into ever who will ever defeat you in a debate again.

Muslims often get saved once they are shown the bankruptcy of their position.

I'm going to list these resources for you now. Remember: "ISBN" stands for International Standard Book Number. Every book that has been professionally published has one. If you know the ISBN of a book, you can find it easily in any book store in the world, or you can special order it.

BOOKS

THE ISLAMIC INVASION
By: Dr. Robert A. Morey
ISBN 193 123 0072

If today I was called upon and asked to teach Christians how to reach out to Muslims, this book would be the assigned text that I'd make my students read. It is the classic work on Islam, and it was the first thing I ever picked up back in 1999 that let me know that Islam can actually be defeated. Muslims can actually be out-debated and shown the deficiencies of their religion. They can be won over to Jesus Christ. It changed my life and prompted me to dig deeper into The Qur'an (my studies ultimately led me to write this book) so I could see its problems for myself. You can become a powerful witness of Christ to Muslims if you know the information contained in this book.

WINNING THE WAR AGAINST RADICAL ISLAM
By: Dr. Robert A. Morey
ISBN 193 123 0080

This book is so controversial that it makes my book look like it is holding back. It is about 250 pages that refute Islam and put forth a specific plan to stop terrorism in America. It goes into greater depth than my book does! Since it is so controversial, your local bookstore may or may not be able to get it. You may have to call the

Christian ministry of the author, called Faith Defenders, in order to obtain your copy. It is 1-800-41-TRUTH. Or you can check him out on the web at www.faithdefenders.com and order it there as well.

ISLAM REVEALED: A CHRISTIAN ARAB'S VIEW OF ISLAM
By: Dr. Anis A. Shorrosh
ISBN 078 526 4647

This book is unique because its author can read and understand Arabic, which is the language that The Qur'an was originally in. So he can really break down some of the problems in it. Also, being from the Middle East, he grew up hearing the best arguments that the Muslim world has to offer. He's heard them all before and can teach you how to answer them. Have you ever been in a debate with a person and known every argument ahead of time that they were going to use, and even had an answer for it waiting for them? It is a great thing. Dr. Shorrosh's book will put you in that position next time a Muslim attacks your faith in Jesus Christ, or next time you're witnessing to a Muslim.

ANSWERING ISLAM: THE CRESCENT IN LIGHT OF THE CROSS
By: Dr. Norman L. Geisler & Abdul Saleeb
ISBN 080 106 4309

This book is devastating to Islam. It answers it really soundly. Dr. Norman L. Geisler is an internationally-known scholar. Abdul Saleeb is a former Muslim who has become a Christian. Together they've made this great book that will help equip you to evangelize the lost Muslims. My favorite section is called "How Muslims Do Apologetics". Have you heard Muslims defend Islam before and they sounded unbeatable? Well, this section teaches you that those arguments are not very good at all. Your library is not complete if this is missing from it.

THE FACTS ON ISLAM
By: John Ankerberg & John Weldon
ISBN 089 081 9130

If you pick up a copy of this one, pick up about 10 and hand them out as Bible tracts. It is a small booklet, but it is jam-packed with the facts. One of the major reasons I did not cave in in 1997 and become a Muslim is because of this booklet. Small, but powerful and effective.

FAST FACTS ON ISLAM
By: John Ankerberg & John Weldon
ISBN 073 691 0115

This one is a little thicker than their previous one. It is a follow-up to their "FACTS ON" book from years earlier. It is good because it tells the truth about Islam, and does not sugar-coat anything. Books of this kind are in short supply. They've done a wonderful job.

THE MOON-gOD ALLAH IN THE ARCHEOLOGY OF THE MIDDLE EAST
By: Dr. Robert A. Morey
No ISBN - Call 1-800-41-TRUTH To Order

Remember earlier on in this book when I called Allah by the name of Al-Ilah, and called him an ancient pagan moon god? Well, this booklet gives you the evidence from archeology that proves it. It is complete with photographs of the idol statues of Al-Ilah with a crescent moon carved on his chest which have been unearthed in Arabia.

The pagan Arabs were worshipping the god of the moon long before Muhammad was even born! Allah is this god, dressed up in different clothes! If you show this to a Muslim, they will know for the first time the truth that they are participating in idol worship.

ISLAM: WHAT YOU NEED TO KNOW
By: Ron Rhodes
ISBN 073 690 2090

This one is a short pamphlet, but is inexpensive and is full of really good information which will teach you things about Islam that you possibly have not known before.

THE ISLAM DEBATE
By: Josh McDowell & John Gilchrist
ISBN 086 605 104X

This book is a written account of the debate between Josh McDowell and Ahmed Deedat. It was given to me as a gift by a concerned Christian friend of mine prior to my salvation who knew that Muslims were approaching me about converting to Islam. Since my Islamic literature was by Deedat, I had great respect for him at that time. When I read the Christian McDowell take him in a debate, my eyes were opened up a little bit more.

When you read these suggested titles, you will be able to dialogue with any Muslim that you could ever meet. Whether he be a Muslim on the street or a college-educated intellect, you will still be able to topple Islam and help point him to Christ.

WEB SITES

www.faithdefenders.com

This is the ministry of Dr. Robert A. Morey. It is called Faith Defenders. He has debated some of the biggest names in the Islamic scholastic world, including Shabir Ali and Dr. Jamal Badawi. These debates still exist on video tape and you can order them. He also has his book "THE ISLAMIC INVASION" in other formats, like video tape and audio tape. These lectures can be a great supplement to the book in helping you learn all you can about Islam.

He has a live call-in radio show called "Bob Morey Live" that has lead to the salvation of Muslims and has warned major cities about attacks before they have happened. If your local Christian radio station does not have this show on its programming line-up, you need to call the station manager and get on him/her about it!

www.impactapologetics.com

This web site features Dr. Norman L. Geisler and other defenders of Christianity. There are various audio-recorded singles and albums with lectures about Islam. They have various books dealing with Islam. Some of their resources have titles like "Answering Islam" and "Answering Muslims' Objections" and "Answering The Threat Of Islam" and "The Testimony Of A Former Muslim" and "Is The Qur'an The Word Of God?" and "Is Muhammad A Prophet Of God?" and "The Islamic Threat" and "The

Islamic View Of Christ" and others! There is a ton of knowledge available to you at this site if you will only visit it and order these things.

www.focusing-on-islam.com

This is the web site of Dr. Anis Shorrosh. His ministry is called "TRUTH IN CRISIS INTERNATIONAL". The resources I recommend you pick up from here are his "ISLAM REVEALED" on audio book if you would like. Also the video tape of his debate with Ahmed Deedat. He also dialogued with Dr. Jamal Badawi on the John Ankerberg Show and that is on video tape as well. He debated Dr. Badawi at the University of Kansas about The Qur'an (and whether it was the word of God), and this is on tape too!

There are a ton of resources on this web site. You need to check it out for yourself.

When you pick up these recommended materials and also check out these web sites, you will be a Christian who is equipped to witness to Muslims. And you will be fearless, knowing that even the Muslims who think they are the greatest will still not be able to shake you in a debate! I hope these resources help you out.

Imagine the impact on our inner-cities and our Muslim communities if *EVERY* Christian got their hands on these things and studied them! Islam would have no one to approach. It could not steal any more Christians out of Christianity. It could not walk around making crazy statements against Christianity un-checked, because the average Christian would be ready and able to refute it.

Muslims would convert by the thousands! People who have been sent over here to hurt our country through acts of terrorism would be converted before they even had the chance to do anything to us!

What are you waiting for? The hour where the Christian church sleeps while Islam plans its next move against America is over! It's time to act! If September 11th, 2001 does not motivate you to want to do something for God about Islam, what will?!

Your education must begin immediately! Pick these things up from the internet or at your local book store and learn what's in them! Teach other Christians what you have learned about reaching Muslims! Then let's all go out with our knowledge and evangelize the lost Muslims! Let's impact our Muslim communities for Christ!

Brian James Shanley

APPENDIX D

Morey's Radical Suggestion - "TOUGH LOVE"

*What you're about to read is an excerpt from the book "**WINNING THE WAR AGAINST RADICAL ISLAM**" by Dr. Robert A. Morey. The book in its entirety can be purchased on www.faithdefenders.com or by calling 1-800-41-TRUTH. Please get your hands on it. The proceeds support his Christian ministry.*

*I've chosen to include his "**Chapter 8: It Is Time For Tough Love**" (pages 167-174) as an appendix to my work because it outlines a plan for counter-acting terrorism that can be put into place by America at the government level. It is not just a plan, but it is a plan that will work! There are nations whose leaders have read his book in its entirety and they are making its suggested changes towards answering Islamic terrorism once and for all. It is my hope that America joins them.*

We are at war. During times of war, we should have no problem "biting the bullet" and being put through a time of slight and temporary inconvenience in order to achieve a greater good - which is the preservation of America as a nation. Those who genuinely care about not getting hit by another September 11th, 2001 attack again will be interested to see the solution.

It is a little wild. It is a little drastic. It is a little radical. It is exactly what we need. And I'm including it because I'm in agreement with it.

The things we've been doing up until now have obviously not been working. A change in approach is needed. And Dr. Morey provides that new approach. He was fighting the war against Islam while I was still playing dodge ball in my kindergarten gym class. He knows what he is talking about.

From here on out, the words you read here until the end of the appendix will be those of Dr. Morey.

[By the way, Dr. Morey is okay with me including this. I consider him a friend and in a way a mentor. He's given me permission to include these pages of his book in my own book.]

Brian James Shanley

IT IS TIME FOR TOUGH LOVE

America is at war whether we like it or not. The days to come do not bode well for the property and lives of Americans overseas or here at home. The specter of a nuclear and biological attack looms large on the horizon. Liberals are more concerned about protecting the feelings of Muslims than protecting the lives of Americans. If loyal Americans do not rise up and demand that the present government fulfill its constitutional duty to protect the lives and property of the citizens of this great land, who will?

This chapter will outline what has to be done internationally and nationally to win the war against Muslim terrorism. If we do not implement this plan, thousands, if not millions, will die.

THE FINAL SOLUTION TO INTERNATIONAL TERRORISM

Is there anything so important to Muslim terrorists such as bin Laden, that in order to save it, they will renounce their Jihad against America? Is there anything so important to Saudi Arabia and other Muslim countries that in order to save it, they will stop supporting terrorism? Do we have any leverage in our war with radical Islam?

Since they are willing to commit suicide and to sacrifice their own family members to achieve their terrorist goals, it would seem that there is nothing so important to them that the mere thought of losing it would bring their Jihad to a halt. But this is not true.

The terrorists and terrorist nations such as Saudi Arabia only fear one thing: *the destruction of the religion of Islam.* There is nothing in this life that has greater value to them than Islam. They are willing to sacrifice and even die to promote Islam. This *religious* motivation is the engine that drives the Jihad against us.

THE ACHILLES HEEL OF ISLAM

The path to Paradise, according to the Five Pillars of Islam, involves the city of Mecca and its stone temple called the Kabah. Muslims pray toward Mecca five times a day. *What if Mecca didn't exist anymore?*

They must make a pilgrimage to Mecca and engage in an elaborate set of rituals centered around the Kabah once they arrive. *What if Mecca and the Kabah were only blackened holes in the ground?*

What if Medina, the burial place of Muhammad was wiped off the face of the planet?

What if the Dome Mosque on the temple site in Jerusalem was blown up?

The greatest weakness of Islam is that it is hopelessly tied to sacred cities and buildings. If these cities and buildings were destroyed, Islam would die within a generation as it would be apparent to all that its god could not protect the three holiest sites in Islam.

The Sword Held Over Their Heads

With American ships stationed all around Arabia and troops on the ground within Saudi Arabia itself, it would take about seven minutes for cruise missiles to take out Mecca and Medina. These cities could be vaporized in minutes and there is nothing that the Saudis or any other Muslim country could do to stop us. The Israelis could take out the Dome Mosque at the same time. It could happen so fast that no one would have the time to respond. With these surgical strikes, few lives would be lost. And with three strikes against them, Islam is out!

The Threat

The US government and its allies must agree that this is the final solution to the Muslim problem. We must tell all terrorist groups that the next time they destroy the lives and property of Americans at home or abroad, we will destroy Mecca, Medina, and the Dome Mosque. They will be responsible for destroying the three most holy sites in Islam and bringing the religion to its knees.

We must tell all the Muslim countries that are presently supporting and harboring terrorists that if they do not cease and desist at once, we will destroy the heart of their religion.

Saudi Arabia and the rest of the Islamic World would, for the first time in their bloody history of oppression and tyranny, have to give civil rights and human rights to women and non-Islamic religions. They would have to allow their people to decide for themselves what religion, if any, they want in their lives. The "religious police" would be disbanded.

All Islamic laws would have to give way to the UN declaration on human rights, civil rights, women's rights, and freedom of religion. Once Muslim governments took their foot off the neck of their people, millions of Muslims would convert to Christianity as they have had enough of oppression and violence from their Imams and Mullahs.

HOME SECURITY

What must we do to catch all the terrorists hiding in this country before they are activated and kill more Americans? Tough love demands that we act swiftly and without any concern for feelings. When people are dying, we do not have the luxury of political correctness. The following steps must be taken at once.

1. Education

No school, college, or university that receives federal or state aid may register or teach any students who do not provide a birth certificate or the appropriate papers proving that they are legal citizens of this country. If a school, college, or university refuses to comply with this requirement, all federal and state aid is to be suspended until they do.

Any students who fail to provide a birth certificate or the papers to prove they are legal immigrants, shall be turned over to the appropriate federal and state authorities to see if the entire family is illegal. If they are all illegal, they must be rounded up, interrogated and, unless they can show due cause, they should be sent back to their home country.

2. Medical Services

All hospitals and doctors must require patients to provide a birth certificate or the appropriate papers proving that they are legal citizens of this country. Since illegal aliens are not citizens, they do not have a right to free medical care. Any and all illegal aliens who apply for medical attention will be turned over to the appropriate federal and state authorities to see if the entire family is illegal. If they are all illegal, they must be rounded up, interrogated and, unless they can show due cause, they should be sent back to their home country.

3. Draft Registration

All males must register for the draft when they reach 18 years of age. At that time, they provide a birth certificate or the appropriate papers proving that they are legal citizens of this country. Any male who fails to provide a birth certificate or the papers to prove he is a legal immigrant, shall be turned over to the appropriate federal and state authorities to see if his entire family is illegal. If they are all illegal, they must be rounded up, interrogated and, unless they can show due cause, they should be sent back to their home country.

4. Employment

All employees must provide a birth certificate or the appropriate papers proving to their employers that they are legal citizens of this country. Anyone who fails to provide a birth certificate or the papers to prove he is a legal immigrant shall be turned over to the appropriate federal and state authorities to see if his entire family is illegal. If they are all illegal, they must be rounded up, interrogated and, unless they can show due cause, they should be sent back to their home country.

5. Police Check Points

In addition to providing car registration and an insurance certificate whenever a vehicle is stopped for any reason, drivers shall also provide a birth certificate or the appropriate papers proving that they are legal citizens of this country. Any driver who fails to provide a birth certificate or the papers to prove he is a legal immigrant shall be turned over to the appropriate federal and state authorities to see if his entire family is illegal. If they are all illegal, they must be rounded up, interrogated and, unless they can show due cause, they should be sent back to their home country.

6. Bank and Stock Information

In addition to a valid Social Security number, anyone seeking to open or maintain a bank account or to use any financial services must provide a birth certificate or the appropriate papers proving that they are legal citizens of this country. Anyone who fails to provide a birth certificate or the papers to prove he is a legal immigrant shall be turned over to the appropriate federal and state authorities to see if his entire family is illegal. If they are all illegal, they must be rounded up, interrogated and, unless they can show due cause, they should be sent back to their home country.

7. Welfare and Unemployment Benefits

All those who apply for welfare or unemployment benefits must provide a birth certificate or the appropriate papers proving that they are legal citizens of this country.

Anyone who fails to provide a birth certificate or the papers to prove he is a legal immigrant, shall be turned over to the appropriate federal and state authorities to see if his entire family is illegal. If they are all illegal, they must be rounded up, interrogated and, unless they can show due cause, they should be sent back to their home country.

8. Immigration

Any citizens, students, or illegal immigrants from Islamic countries that are listed by the State Department as being a terrorist state, must report for registration and interrogation. Anyone who fails to provide a birth certificate or the papers to prove he is a legal immigrant, shall be turned over to the appropriate federal and state authorities to see if his entire family is illegal. It they are all illegal, they must be rounded up, interrogated and, unless they can show due cause, they should be sent back to their home country.

9. Military Service

Since several terrorists received their training in the U.S. military, all Muslim military personnel and Muslim chaplains must be deemed as a security risk and not allowed access to sensitive information or to weapons of mass destruction.

10. Mosques and Islamic Information Centers

All mosques and Islamic centers must provide all financial records of any and all funds sent outside of this country. If full disclosure reveals that a Mosque or an

Islamic Center sent money to any terrorist cause or group, they are to be shut down as agents of a foreign power. In America, people are free to believe whatever they want. But they are not free to seek the overthrow of the government or to destroy the property and lives of those who disagree with them.

11. The Intelligence Community

The FBI, the CIA, and other intelligence agencies of the United States shall be given full power to infiltrate Muslim charitable groups, mosques, schools, and centers and to seek the identity of anyone who supports terrorism by any means deemed necessary.

CONCLUSION

If these ten measures are adopted and put into action, within two years America will be a safe place to live and work. If they are not adopted, then the terrorists will have the freedom to destroy the lives and property of Americans at will.

These steps will be taken now or later. Once a nuclear or bio-chemical holocaust is unleashed against America, people will be ready for tough love. But why wait until millions of Americans are dead or dying before doing what we all know must be done to protect this land?

ABOUT THE AUTHOR

Brian James Shanley was born in 1976 in Minnesota, USA. He graduated from Roosevelt High School in Minneapolis in 1995. He converted to Christianity in 1998. In 2000, he completed the requirements necessary to earn a 2-year degree in Biblical Studies. It is his goal to return to school in the future to further his education, as God provides the opportunity and funds.

In 2000-2001, he served as the Assistant to the Youth Director at Bethesda Missionary Baptist Church in Minneapolis, and was involved in equipping young Christians for works of service to God.

As it stands right now in 2002, he teaches occasionally at *YHWH Church of God In Christ* in Minneapolis. If you're in MN, call there on 612-825-7877 to find out when he is teaching next.

Prior to "*MANHATTAN MASSACRE*", Shanley has authored a few unpublished papers, tracts, and booklets and has recorded a few Christian audio taped Bible lessons. But this is his first published work.

He currently resides in The Twin Cities, MN, USA with his child. There he is working on his next book, which he also plans to publish in the future.

Brian James Shanley can be contacted on 612-867-0699 via voicemail. He loves feedback from his readers. As a show of gratitude for your support in having purchased this book, he will gladly sign your copy of this book if you mail it to him. His P.O. Box address, email address, and any other contact information that he sets up in the future will be recited on the greeting of his voice mail box. Call and listen for them!

THANK YOU'S

I told myself that I was not going to do anything like this, because I'd list a bunch of people that have been there for me and I'd accidentally miss someone. But I'm going to go for it anyways. If you were there for me and I missed you, please know that it was a total accident. Just make me aware, and I'll get you on the next one.

First and foremost, I'd like to thank the God of The Bible, Who exists simultaneously as Father, Son, and Holy Spirit. You're the reason why I've had the strength to go on living. You've come through for me more times than I can even count. Even after having bailed me out of everything before this, You have still seen fit to move me along to finish this book. I submit to Your calling over my life. Thanks. May You be praised forever.

Thank you to my mother Susan Thorp and her husband Brad. As a family, we've had our ups and downs, our sunny days and our cloudy days. But through it all we are still close. Thanks for seeing what I was trying to accomplish through my book, even though the world around me thought I was some evil jerk for writing it.

To my little princess, Gabrielle, I want to say that you are a miracle from God. I love you more than I love my own life. As I am writing this right now, you are only 4 years old. One day you'll be old enough to read what your daddy has written for you. Since the months before your birth, I've sacrificed all things to make sure that you are properly

*taken care of. I would do it all again if I had to, because .
you mean everything to me. Thank you for being born.*

*To Keiasha Hill, there will come a day when you are old
enough to read these words. We do not have the chance to
see each other, and I do not have a chance to help you out.
I want you to know that it is not my doing, but the doing of
other people. I pray for you every night, and I will always
be here for you. No matter how many years pass by, the
door will not ever be closed.*

*Thanks to Cary Malaske (hi, Corinne). You are the only
dad that I have ever known. Biologically, I was not your
responsibility. But it did not stop you from loving me and
being there for me. Words cannot express what it did for
me to have you around in my life. Even after you and my
mother went your separate ways, you kept on taking care of
me! I shudder to think about how I would have turned out if
I did not have you as I grew up. Thanks for being there.*

*To the entire Malaske family, thanks for being behind Cary
in his decision to raise another man's kid. No one could
ever tell that I am not blood-related to you guys, because
you've treated me like I was family my whole life.*

*Thanks to the entire Shanley family and all of their in-laws.
You know you are too numerous to mention individually, so
I am not even going to try. Just want to say thanks for
being sympathetic to me as I grew up through hard times.
And thanks for being behind me, even when I've done things
that you did not all agree with. I'd especially like to thank
my aunt Sandra Crouch for bailing me out of trouble, even
trouble I created for myself.*

To my sister Tara Jones, we have experienced both triumph and tragedy together and I think it has made us close. I love you.

To the entire Jones family, thank you for treating me like one of your own. I still feel like I am one of your own.

To my inner circle of friends, Justin Kidd, Cameron Dronen, and Joe Ervin (and I cannot forget about Mrs. Joe Ervin either), all I can say is that you've all had my back through some of the worst storms that this life can throw at a person. God has used you all in my life, and you are part of the reason I'm still standing. I have not always acted the way I should, but you've stayed by me through it all. We've all been friends for over a decade now. I hope that we're all tight for decades to come as well.

To my sister, Heather Malaske, and her daughter Aliyana (my niece), thanks for your help in the area of my daughter. Being a single parent is difficult, but when you're surrounded by family like you two, it helps out a great deal.

To James Hunter at The Twin Cities Bible Institute, thanks for being not only a teacher, but a counselor and a friend. The fact that I was saved and grew under your teaching means that you played a role, to a degree, in my authorship of this book. And whatever I do in the future for God, you played a role in that as well. I know you will be rewarded accordingly.

To Jeff Vahl, Bob Hazard, Dr. Raymond Buck (one of the key people who inspired me to evangelize people trapped in false religions) and Dr. Roy Beacham, also at The Twin Cities Bible Institute, thanks for your contributions to my growth as a believer. And thanks for being available after class hours to address some of my questions. I still have more, so I'll still be calling you at times.

To Elder Kevin Wilson and his wife Crystal, I'd like to give a big acknowledgement as well. After my car died, you've made extra stops out of your way just to transport myself and my little girl to church. Thank you.

To Winston Allen, thank you for encouraging me during hard times. You have been involved in church longer than I have been alive. And it is refreshing and beautiful to see a brother still as zealous and ready to witness for the truth as you are. No matter how dark it looks, never let the world beat that out of you.

To Mr. Rev. Samuel Reuben, thanks for being there for me and listening to my problems when it seemed like the world was falling apart around me. You are surrounded by people who do not understand the gift that they have in the fact that they know you. Never let false testimony or someone's personal problems against you get you down. We serve a God of perfect justice who will right every wrong that has been done to you.

To the church family at YHWH Church of God in Christ, thank all of you for using me in the area of my spiritual gift and also for edifying me through the exercise of your own gifts. I know that our church is going to do greater things in the community in the future than we ever have before, and I'm excited about that.

To Maxine Thompson, thanks for being my friend at a time in my life when I did not know who to trust. You're a strong young mother, and I see in you the drive and the ability to do right by your daughter.

To Liberty Chari, thank you for listening as I've "sounded off" about many issues. May you never lose sight of the idea that absolute truth exists. And may you seek to understand The Gospel fully, and fully experience what it can do for you.

Michelle Cobb, thank you. When I look at a young believer being excited to tear into The Bible, it personally challenges me to regain the same zeal. Don't ever stop wanting everyone to know about Jesus, and don't ever stop trying to tell them the truth.

To Dr. Bob Morey, thanks for allowing me to borrow a few pages from your book. You were answering Islam and warning America while I was still learning my alphabet and numbers in kindergarten. Your ministry has played a major role in my development and growth as a Christian. I hope that at The Judgment Seat you are rewarded not only for helping me out, but also for any lives I am eventually used by God to touch as well.

Thanks to Rev. Brett O'Neill and the rest of the O'Neill family in Wisconsin. It was not an accident that we all have met, and it was not an accident that I've moved about a million times and we've still been able to be in contact. God has kept you through some really hard times. And you've been used to by Him to make a contribution to my spiritual growth.

To Elder Brett McNeill (not to be confused with Rev. Brett O'Neill above), thanks for allowing me to work in the vineyard at the church.

To my people at Eschelon Telecom - especially Manny Gutierrez, Mandy Nallick, Sean Schaefer, Loren Kelly, Winston Butler, Tom Davis, Tijuana Hawkins, Jason Linehan, Alex Beberman, Mark Mancini, Dan Oberpriller, and Jonathan Morris - I told you I had a book coming out soon! Now you believe me, huh? Thanks for reading various rough drafts and giving me your opinions. Thanks also for seeing where I was going with this project, and why it is so important.

Thanks to Rev. Arthur Agnew of Bethesda Missionary Baptist Church. Your style of in-your-face, tell it like it is, never compromising the truth no matter what the circumstances preaching made a gigantic impact on me, the way I teach, and the way I write. I needed to hear it. I am glad to have come under your kind of preaching early on instead of any of the alternatives that are out there. Could you imagine if I had started out in a "seeker sensitive" church or something? Thanks for being a bold lion of the faith. It was a wonderful model of preaching for me to be exposed to early on, and it will stay with me for the rest of my life.

And finally, thank you to all of you, the readers, who have supported me by purchasing this book. I would not be anywhere without you! I hope you have learned from it, and it has shown you a view of this situation that you maybe have never thought about before. I hope you will support me in the future when I publish more writings.

If you know someone else who could benefit from the information contained in this book, please purchase additional copies at <u>www.1stbooks.com</u>. It would be a great issue to study at your group Bible Study, Sunday School, or Current Events class at school!

If I owe you a thank-you and I have missed you, I'm asking you to please forgive me. It was an honest accident. Please let me know, and I'll get you in my next one.

Brian James Shanley
2002

Printed in the United States
971400005B/193-222